CHASING TIGER

Also by Glenn Stout

Red Sox Century

CHASING TIGER

THE TIGER WOODS READER

edited by **Glenn Stout**

DA CAPO PRESS

A list of copyright acknowledgments appears on page 211.

Chasing Tiger: The Tiger Woods Reader is a work of journalism which has not been authorized, licensed or endorsed by either Tiger Woods or the Tiger Woods Foundation.

Designed by Jeffrey P. Williams
Set in 12-point Goudy by the Perseus Books Group

Cataloging-in-Publication data for this book is available from the Library of Congress.

First Da Capo Press edition 2002
ISBN 0–306–81124–3

Published by Da Capo Press
A Member of the Perseus Books Group
http://www.dacapopress.com

Da Capo Press books are available at special discounts for bulk purchases in the U.S. by corporations, institutions, and other organizations. For more information, please con-tact the Special Markets Department at the Perseus Books Group, 11 Cambridge Cen-ter, Cambridge, MA 02142, or call (800) 255-1514 or (617) 252-5298, or e-mail j.mccrary@perseusbooks.com.

1 2 3 4 5 6 7 8 9—06 05 04 03 02

CONTENTS

INTRODUCTION

Glenn Stout

Tiger Woods is only twenty-six years old, still a young man, an unfinished piece. As a persona and an athlete one must presume he is still closer to the beginning than the end, and that his story is far from over. And despite playing a game that is less familiar to most residents of the world than many others, for more than twenty years – since the age of *five* – writers have looked at Tiger Woods, watched what he has done, and tried to capture him with words.

As I write this, over the last two decades more than 1,400 stories about Tiger Woods that have appeared in major American magazines. This doesn't include the thousands and thousands of stories that have appeared in newspapers, the thousands more that have appeared in publications elsewhere in the world, or those that merely make mention of Woods and his deeds in passing. No, these

1,400 stories are all about Woods himself – who he is, what he has done, and what that might mean. He may well be one of the most written about human beings on the planet.

He has proven to be an elusive target. As soon as he has been identified as one thing, he has metamorphosed into something else, moving from prodigy to prodigal son to product, from symbol to sensation and savior almost seamlessly, evolving as the intense light of scrutiny waxes and wanes with each word.

Beyond the obvious skills of writing and reporting, the stories in this book have been selected for the way the way their authors have responded to Woods. Each not only sees something different in Woods, but each sees him differently, from a different place. Woods was first viewed as some kind of exotic wunderkind – but not just young and not even entirely African-American, but an entire African, Caucasian, Thai, Chinese and Cherokee melting pot. As his accomplishments became more tangible and pronounced, writers have followed him to places beyond the golf course and back again. They continue to explore him beyond questions of age, race and sport. In their skillful hands the best golfer the planet has ever seen is also considered as a social and political symbol, huckster, sex object and icon of various kinds. Their stories serve as a kind of evolving definition of Woods, a living biography that tells us about him and the various worlds he inhabits.

This is a challenge, and that is one reason why writers have found him such an intriguing subject. That, and the cold hard fact that Tiger sells and people yearn to know him. Television ratings double when he is in a tournament. Newsstand sales of magazines featuring Woods on the cover skyrocket. According to a Gallup poll in June of 2000 – before Woods completed his "Tiger Slam"—fully 88% of Americans look upon him favorably, more than any other athlete. Ever. That is an amazing number for anyone notable for any reason, but an incredible one for a person whose notoriety stems from his ability to make a golf ball go where he wants it to go.

Yet I suspect this may actually be the reason so many are attracted to him. Not because he can make a golf ball go where he wants it to, but because in doing so he exhibits an element of control that seems beyond us. He sees exactly what he must do and then does it, instantly and almost effortlessly, time and time again. It is "just" golf, but it sometimes seems as if golf is really incidental to this greater gift.

That is what intrigues me. I am not much of a golfer, but I watch Tiger Woods, and not just on Sunday during the final round when he is in contention. There have been Thursday mornings when I have sat with coffee and watched him play overseas, and Friday afternoons I have knocked off early to watch him in Milwaukee or California, Saturdays when I've missed a train home and sat with strangers in a bar because Woods is making a charge and none of us can pull ourselves away. Because when he is playing well there is nothing else in sports quite like it. Most athletes speak of getting into "the zone," where time slows and they are able to accomplish feats that are usually much more difficult, if not impossible. Even for the best, such times are usually fleeting, lasting only a few moments. Only on the rarest of occasions, for the rarest of athletes, do these moments last an entire game or day. For Tiger Woods these moments sometimes last months.

This leaves me dumbfounded. I sometimes wonder if he is really that good, or if golf is actually quite easy and an entire industry has been pulling off a grand deception, a conspiracy lasting generations, one that only Woods, for some clandestine reason, has been allowed to expose. I even wonder if that is why there are times he does not play well, sometimes for months, just to extend that deception and build our anticipation for the moment when it appears again.

As fascinating as it has been to watch Woods play, it has been equally fascinating to watch Tiger Woods emerge through the words he has inspired, an experience that is the goal of this collection. To most of the general sports audience he exploded with little advance warning; one day he was just suddenly *there*, the best golfer in the world. But those of us who spend too much of our time reading about sports have been periodically reading about Woods for over twenty years. That now makes it worthwhile to look back and see what the writers have seen, for their words provide an opportunity to track his evolution. The first few times Woods was noticed in print, while not substantive enough to bear repeating in this collection, are nevertheless worth mentioning. The Tiger Woods we know today was already present. We can already recognize him.

The first notable mention of Woods in a national magazine took place on page 21 of the November 1981 issue of *Golf Digest*, in a small story of several paragraphs entitled "5-Year-Old Tiger – He's Incredible." He shares the page with another feature on Eberhard Steiniger, the retired course superintendent at New Jersey's Pine Valley, who says of his old course, "No one is shamed to shoot 105 here."

But the story on Woods sits atop the page. He is described as "as tall as a ball washer," and the story outlines the now-familiar details of his upbringing, such as watching his father practice from his high chair and hitting balls in the garage while still a toddler. We learn that he has already won more than a dozen trophies, shot an eighteen-hole 57 at the par–3 Heartwell Golf Park, and that Heartwell golf pro Rudy Duran finds him "not exceptional . . . [but] phenomenal." No kidding. Tiger, the story notes, has already appeared on television several times, but is already nonplused about his celebrity status. "Golfers get on television lots of times," he says confidently, as if knowing what his future holds. One gets the distinct impression that had he been asked, the five-year-old Tiger would have admitted to being ashamed to shoot a 105 at Pine Valley.

Ebony found him a year later, in another brief story entitled "A Golfing Champion at Six." By this ripe age Woods also admits to enjoying bicycles and cartoons, but we learn that he is already out-putting his father and that Duran now believes he might be playing on the pro tour at age fifteen. But what is most remarkable is a three-picture triptych of Woods's swinging, resplendent in black and white saddle shoes. Well, I'm not Butch Harmon, but the six-year-old's swing is a dead ringer for that of the twenty-six-year-old.

Over the next decade Woods's accomplishments in junior golf were occasionally outlined in Southern California newspapers and mentioned in golf publications, but his next notable appearance in print came in *Sports Illustrated* on September 24, 1990, in the familiar "Faces in the Crowd" feature. Along with a ten-year-old swimming champion, a twenty-four-year-old weight-lifting chemist and the fifty-six year old race walker, we find fourteen-year old Woods, noted for his five Junior World titles and recent tournament win in Fort Worth, Texas. The story is notable only because it would be the last time that Woods would ever be considered just another "face in the crowd." For after that comes the deluge, beginning with Jaime Diaz's profile from the *New York Times* in 1991, the story that begins this collection.

Even in these first, brief stories, the pattern was set, the path of Tiger already marked out. What may be most remarkable is that Woods has actually proceeded in that direction and even exceeded those early prophecies. His talent was indeed "phenomenal," and Woods was correct that golfers would be on television all the time, particularly after he arrived. And although he was not on the pro tour at age fifteen, as a sixteen-year-old amateur he did compete in his first professional tournament, the Los Angeles Open at Riviera. The other "Faces in the Crowd" profiled that day in *Sports Illustrated* have returned to anonymity. One can imagine that page preserved in their scrapbooks for-ever, once because of what they accomplished themselves, but now perhaps because they shared a page with young Mr. Woods as a relative equal. Woods, however, has since made the move from a face in the crowd to become the face the crowd seeks out. As demonstrated herein, at each step since there are more of us—fans and writers—chasing after him.

The actual tiger, *pantherus tigris*, provides an interesting metaphor for the *homo sapien* Tiger due to its particular form of camouflage, which neither disguises the animal as something else nor mimics its background. The tiger's stripes represent what naturalists refer to as "disruptive" camouflage. Their coloration and design combine to dis-rupt the tiger's outline, making it nearly undetectable. When one looks at a tiger, our eyes do not easily translate the pattern of stripes and shades of black and tan and white and brown into the outline of the animal, particularly when it knows that we are watching and stays very still. Woods, like the tiger, has the ability to be both present while still not fully revealing.

As I created this collection, I often thought of this, for it seems to me that this is another reason why Woods has attracted such interest from writers and such a variety of approaches. They are all trying to see Tiger Woods, and his camouflage is no less disruptive. His youth, talent, ethnic-ity, money, and power somehow combine to place him just out of reach. The writers circle and track but Woods still eludes them, escaping from the net of words they have created. He is not just the prodigy, not just the product, and not just the symbol. Just when he seems unbeatable, he loses. Just when he threatens to become "just" another golfer, albeit a very good one, he provides a transcendent moment. No one writer has yet captured this outline whole, but through their combined portraiture in this volume, the outline becomes much clearer.

In certain parts of India, woodcutters and others have long entered the tiger's domain at extreme risk, in constant fear of being attacked. After years of study animal behaviorists took note of the manner of these attacks and came up with a solution that has since saved many lives. Those who enter the tiger's realm now wear masks on the back of their heads with large, unblinking eyes.

No one who now competes against Tiger Woods does so without wearing a similar competitive mask. Even as they try to forge ahead and ignore his position on the leader board, they are constantly on alert. Whether they admit to it or not, they often try to make shots they otherwise would not attempt simply because they know that Tiger Woods is present, *somewhere*.

His remarkable talent makes him impossible to ignore. And so, like his competitors, we continue the chase, not yet knowing where he might lead us.

FORE! NICKLAUS
BEWARE OF TEEN-AGER

Jaime Diaz

While Jack Nicklaus was adding another laurel to the greatest career in golf with his victory at the United States Senior Open last weekend, the most precocious golfer in the modern history of the game gained his greatest victory.

At the age of 15 years 7 months, Eldrick (Tiger) Woods became the youngest winner in the 44-year history of the United States Junior Amateur championship on Sunday, sweeping through six match-play victories at the Bay Hill Club in Orlando, Fla.

Woods is the first black to win the junior championship, and joins Alton Duhon, who won the United States Senior

Amateur in 1982, and William A. Wright, who won the United States Amateur Public Links in 1959, as the only blacks ever to win American National Championships.

Expectations Are High

Greatness has been expected for Woods since the age of 3, when he shot 48 for nine holes on the regulation length Navy Golf Club near his Cypress, Calif., home. His unabashed ambition, after completing his amateur and college career, is to become the game's dominant player.

"I want to become the Michael Jordan of golf," said Woods, who prefers being called Tiger to Eldrick. "I'd like to be the best ever."

To keep himself on track, Woods keeps a piece of paper in his bedroom that documents Niclaus's feats from the age of 10. Woods broke 80 and 70 before Nicklaus, who never went farther than the semifinals in four attempts at the Junior Amateur. Woods was a semifinalist last year, the first time he played in the championship.

Woods, who will begin 10th grade at Western High School in Anaheim, Calif., in September, took top individual honors in the California high school championships as a freshman in May and won the Los Angeles junior championship in June. The week before coming to Orlando, he won the Optimist Junior World in San Diego in the 15–17 age group, giving him his record sixth age-group victory in that tournament.

A Bobby Jones Pace

But with his victory last weekend, Woods further established himself as the most advanced adolescent golfer since Bobby Jones, who won the Georgia State Amateur at the age of 14.

"I haven't really had time to think about what it means," said Woods yesterday by telephone from Santee, Calif., where he is playing in a junior team championship. "The pressure was awesome, and I was so tired I couldn't talk afterward."

Woods is still filling out at 6 feet and 138 pounds, but he plays power golf. He was consistently 25 yards longer off the tee than his opponents, and showed a professional touch with high, soft-landing iron shots. Over essentially the same course that is host to the PGA Tour's Nestlé Invitational, Woods was the leading qualifying medalist with a four-under-par 140 in 36 holes.

In his final match, against Brad Zwetschke of Kankakee, Ill., Woods fell three down after six holes, but battled back to stand 1 up on the 18th tee. He sharply hooked his drive out of bounds on the 441-yard par 4, lost the hole and sent the match into sudden death.

"It was just the pressure," said Woods, who also hit an iron shot out of bounds on the 13th hole. "I never dreamed that the pressure would be this great."

But Woods, whose caddie, Jay Brunza, also serves as his sports psychologist, composed himself for the playoff and won the championship when Zwetschke missed a 4-foot putt for a bogey.

"I just forgot about what I did on 18 and worried about my tee shot," said Woods. "I try to think one shot at a time."

Matching Shots With Bob Hope

Indeed, Woods acts as if he is immune to the incumbent pressures that often threaten, and sometimes destroy, prodigies. His exploits have received media attention since he was 3 years old, when he competed with Bob Hope in a putting contest on "The Mike Douglas Show."

Woods's most immediate problem is staying rested between tournaments, which number about 30 a year. "School, golf, sleep. That's my life," he said. His father, Earl Woods, a contracts administrator for McDonnell Douglas, often travels with his son and wants to be sure Tiger doesn't lose his love for the game.

"I don't fear burnout, because nothing can replace the joy of winning," said Tiger. "Just that joy of beating every-one in the field. Nothing I could do in life is more fun than that."

By virtue of winning in Orlando, Woods qualified for his first United States Amateur, which begins Aug. 20 at the Honors Course in Ooltewah, Tenn. The defending champion is 21-year-old Phil Mickelson, who for all his youthful prowess, which already includes a PGA Tour Victory, never won the national junior championship.

"Tiger would like to become the first man ever to win the U.S. Junior, Amateur, Open and Senior championships, something even Nicklaus hasn't done," said his father, a former Green Beret. "I know Phil wants to repeat, but he might just run into a Tiger."

New York Times, August 1, 1991

A ZONE OF HIS OWN

Peter de Jonge

On a mild morning in late fall, Tiger Woods, a tall, thin, impossibly elegant Stanford freshman, is standing at the edge of the 17th green of the notorious Shoal Creek golf club near Birmingham, Ala., awaiting his turn to putt. For Woods, who is almost invariably the longest off the tee, and very often the closest to the flag, waiting may be his most characteristic mode, and as he plucks his shirt from his chest, nudges up the bill of his cap with one fingertip, leans on his putter and crosses his legs, each gesture is pared to the nub and full of portent.

What makes his magisterial focus so riveting is the array of reasons he has to feel uneasy. They include, in no particular order, that with just over one hole to play in the Jerry Pate National Intercollegiate, one of the most prestigious tournaments in college golf, he is tied for the lead; that two members of a black activist organization have set up shop outside the golf club's tall iron gates to protest Woods's refusal to boycott the tournament; and that standing just off the green, in jacket and tie and a floppy yellow hat shading a bulbous nose mapped with hundreds of exploded red capillaries, is Hall Thompson, Shoal Creek's 71-year-old founder, who in 1990, just before the P.G.A. Championship here, assured a reporter that his club "don't discriminate in every other area except the blacks."

None of this holds a fly's worth of distraction to Woods, as he calmly looks over the 60 feet of double-humped green. Then again, he is used to dealing with far more expectation and distraction than has ever been dropped upon a single athletic head. While Woods's renown got a big push in the summer, when he became the youngest U.S. Amateur champion (he turned 19 in December), he has been winning world titles since he was 8. Stanford University, which recruited him vigorously and gave him a full scholarship, includes a two-page "Tiger Woods At-a-Glance" flier in its press kit, and the first heading is "Ages 2–5." No less a golfer than Tom Watson calls Woods "potentially the most important player to enter the game in 50 years."

Along the way, the cult has been tirelessly maintained by Tiger's 62-year-old father, Earl Woods, who seems to have conceived of his son's golfing career even before he helped conceive his son. As Tiger left the clubhouse for the final 18 holes of the U.S. Amateur, the last thing Earl whispered in his ear was, "Let the legend grow."

Through the first 53 holes at Shoal Creek, he has displayed every facet of his shimmering teen-age game, from his prodigious drives and world-class putting to the towering long irons that are often compared to Jack Nicklaus's. On the few par 5's where it was worth his while, the 6-foot–2, 150-pound Woods hit drives that carried well over 300 yards. The rest of the time, he relied on a new pet shot, which he calls a "bump driver." "What you do is move close to the ball, and just turn through it, with almost no release or hands," Woods says. "It's a very dead, soft shot, like playing downwind, but it goes straight."

Even rarer than Woods's ability to shape golf shots is his ability to shape the input and output of his mind. Perhaps because there is such an absurd number of things Woods is better off not thinking about, he has developed the Zen-like skill of detaching his brain from his game. "You ever go up to a tee and say, 'Don't hit it left, don't hit it right'?" Woods quizzes me. "That's your conscious mind. My body knows how to play golf. I've trained it to do that. It's just a matter of keeping my conscious mind out of it."

To play the game one shot at a time, unhaunted by your mishaps and unexcited by your feats, is golf's impossible self-selflessness riddle. At Shoal Creek, at least, Woods does an unnerving impression of someone who has cracked it. After the tournament, when he is asked by a local reporter to describe his three rounds, he replies, "I played exactly the same all three rounds." And, amazingly, he had.

Woods's mind control is at least in part a result of his precocious start. Earl Woods believed that if talented athletes were exposed to the game early enough, they would be able to avoid the self-consciousness so common to golfers and perform with the instinctive verve of great basketball and baseball players. In other words, golfers could learn to play like real athletes. "I used to tell people that the next generation of great golfers are going to be those who were introduced to the game between 6 months and a year," Earl says.

That's why Earl, who didn't take up the game until he was 42 but was playing to a 1 handicap within five years, dragged his son's highchair into the garage where Tiger could watch him hit balls into a net. Earl claims that at 6 months, Tiger had an attention span of about two hours, and that when he finally crawled down to take his own turn at the practice mat, he had already absorbed the basic principles of the swing. "His first swing was a perfect imitation of mine," Earl says.

Over the years, Tiger's game has become so ingrained that even under great pressure he can operate on what Earl calls "automatic procedure." There have been times after a round when Earl has asked Tiger how he executed a certain shot, and Tiger says he doesn't know, and others when he can't even recall making contact with the ball.

The depth of Woods's concentration is particularly striking on the greens, where Woods has gone through the same pre-putt routine since he was 6. A few summers ago, Charlie Sifford, the first black regular on the P.G.A. Tour, came out to watch Tiger at a tournament in Texas. At one green, Earl turned his back to Tiger and began a hushed play-by-play for Sifford: "He takes one practice stroke, he takes another. He looks at the target, he looks at the ball. He takes another look at the target, he looks at the ball." And when Earl said "impact" at the exact instant Tiger's putter met the ball, all Sifford could say was, "Goddamn."

This is not to suggest that Woods's play is robotic. His movement is graceful and athletic in the extreme. But his detachment brings an exceptional serenity and inevitability to the whole enterprise. Woods exudes the pure focus and purposefulness of a sleepwalker making his way through the dark to the refrigerator. It's as if he has already made the shot or sunk the key putt, and all that remains is the minor technicality of the present catching up with the reality.

Back on the par–5 17th at Shoal Creek, Woods's 60-foot putt goes up and over the second mound and, after describing a big left-to-right break, comes to rest less than three feet from the hole. Woods calmly knocks it in to go one stroke ahead of his teammate William Yanagisawa. With Thompson standing behind his shoulder, Woods bumps his drive down the 18th fairway and follows it with a short iron to the center of the green. From there he will roll in a 20-foot birdie for a two-shot victory.

As he makes his way up the final fairway, a man standing on a distant terrace silhouetted against Double Oak Mountain fills the basin with an enormous rebel yell of "Go Tiger!" Momentarily diverted from his thoughts—or the absence of them—Woods lets a shy, bucktoothed grin crease his small round face.

Two weeks after Shoal Creek, Earl Woods, an ex-Green Beret who survived several tours of Vietnam before retiring as a lieutenant colonel, and his wife, Kultida Woods, whom he met in Bangkok, are sitting in their living room in Cypress, Calif., 40 miles south of Los Angeles. They are describing the point at which their personal project to raise the greatest golfer who ever lived took on the righteous fervor of a crusade.

When Eldrick Woods was born in 1975 (his much-preferred nickname is in honor of one of his father's Vietnamese war buddies), Earl and Tida agreed that Earl would keep his job as a contracts administrator at McDonnell Douglas and that Tida would stay home. And that when Tiger was old enough to begin playing national junior tournaments, Earl would retire and Tida would go back to work. When Earl and Tiger began their barnstorming six years ago, they flew in the morning of an event, stumbled out for the opening round without sleep or a practice round, then checked into a Motel 6.

"One day, Tiger said, 'Pop, do you think we could get to the site early enough so I could get in a practice round?'" Earl recalls. "I thought about it, and I said: 'Son, I apologize. I promise you from this day forward, you will have just as good of a chance as any of these country club kids, and if I have to go broke, that's what we're going to do.' From that point on, we went a day in advance, he stayed with his peers at the Marriotts and the Hiltons, and he kicked butt and took names."

For Earl Woods, the matter of separate accommodations had a particularly sour resonance. As the first black baseball player at Kansas State University, and, Woods says, in the entire Big Eight Conference, he often had to stay by himself at black hotels and eat in the parking lot while his teammates were inside a restaurant. "We didn't want Tiger to grow up with an inferiority complex," Tida says in her still-thick Thai accent. "So even if we have to take out second mortgage or home equity loan, we let him have it."

As Earl, sucking on Merit 100's, describes the time that the 3-year-old Tiger shot a 48 for nine holes, or he sank 80 four-foot putts in a row, he can sound like every other father of an athletic prodigy, operating in the foggy zone between visionary and madman. What distinguishes Earl is his conviction that, simply by nurturing a young black golfer, he is subverting the racial order.

Until Tiger, black golfers who made a mark have been miracles of self-creation, thorny characters with caddyshack swings who somehow overcame every disadvantage in terms of instruction, facilities and competition. Sifford, who in the 1950's almost single-handedly challenged the P.G.A.'s whites-only clause, wasted a decade of his prime as the personal golf tutor for the band leader Billy Eckstine. Calvin Peete, who won 11 P.G.A. events in the mid–80's, didn't take up the game until he was 23.

Woods, on the other hand, has been raised as a kind of single-case experiment in equal-opportunity indulgence. He has received all the excessive advantages that have routinely been bestowed on white prodigies from Nicklaus and Watson to Phil Mickelson and Ernie Els, current pros whose fathers deemed it necessary to install backyard putting greens.

Woods has been burnished and refined and tweaked to the very limits of his father's credit rating. The care and feeding of his game and mind have been entrusted to a hierarchy of professionals called Team Tiger. It includes Butch Harmon, the distinguished Houston-based swing doctor, and Capt. Jay Brunza, a Navy doctor who has doubled as Woods's sports psychologist and caddy (for major tournaments) since Woods was 13.

On a Friday night in early December, Woods was grabbed from behind in the parking lot behind his Stanford dorm. The mugger held a knife to Woods's throat, called him by name, then turned the knife around and punched him in the face with the handle. When I spoke to Earl Woods the next day, he told me that he had already assigned the mental aspect of the incident to Brunza. "They were able to work through the crisis trauma structure that was already in place to relieve any anxiety he might have had," Earl said. "As a matter of fact, the next day he took a final exam and did very well. He was able to focus." (Woods was only slightly bruised by the blow; the mugger has not been arrested.)

Newspaper articles about Woods often imply that this preternaturally composed young man has benefited from a military-style upbringing, but Earl's parenting style is more

Mr. Rogers than Great Santini. By the time Tiger was born, his father (who has three grown children from a previous marriage) was well into his 40's and retired from the military; the two have the kind of unambivalent, unharried relationship more common between a grandfather and a grandson. "Tiger has never been disciplined, never even been told what to do," Earl says, and then refers to a period very early in their relationship, "when I earned Tiger's respect, and he earned mine." Asked what he respects so much about his father, Tiger says, "Everything." Asked if he can be a little more specific, he says: "I basically respect everything he does. We're best friends."

One of the few issues on which they diverge is race. For Tiger, golf is all that matters, and the news media's constant harping on his race is belittling. For Earl, golf and race cannot be separated. "I told him straight out when he was a little boy," Earl says, "that in America, if you have a drop of black blood in you, you're black." But Tiger, besides Thai, also has Chinese, white and American Indian blood, and doesn't identify himself with one race more than another.

It's a familiar pattern—the father determined to do everything he can to prevent his son from being tainted by the prejudice he has had to deal with, and doing such a good job that the son doesn't see what all the fuss is about.

One of Woods's Stanford teammates is a highly ranked golfer named Notah Begay 3d, who is half Pueblo and half Navajo and is as self-consciously infatuated with his racial heritage as Woods is unintrigued by his own. Before the team headed to Alabama, Begay spoke with Woods about the political significance of Shoal Creek (which, in Woods's honor, he rechristened "Soul Creek").

"I told him," says Begay, who wears a big golf hoop earring, two dabs of red clay on his cheeks and black Oakley shades when he plays, "what a great slap in the face it would be to those who think that minorities are inferior, if he went down and won."

Before the tournament, when I asked Woods if the racist policies at certain country clubs provide a special incentive, he answered no. His father insists otherwise. "Of course it does," he says. "It provides drive. It provides inspiration. It provides motivation. It provides toughness."

And so it appears that Earl Woods has nurtured an almost perfect competitive psyche—one that combines the insider's absolute sense of entitlement with an outsider's private smoldering edge.

The racial significance of what Woods may one day accomplish—the P.G.A. has had precious few black golfers and not a single black superstar—was not lost on the many black employees working the grounds of the plantation-style Shoal Creek. As Woods and the workers crossed paths during his rounds, they would often approach him and quietly pass along their encouragement. And at the start of the final round, a group of caddies, all of them black, came out to see him off the first tee.

When I interview Woods a couple of weeks later in the clubhouse of the Stanford golf course, he is less forthcoming in an hour and a half than in the occasional momentary exchanges we had on the fairway at Shoal Creek. Arriving exactly on time in a black windbreaker and black shorts, his short hair gelled back, he carries himself with the same exaggerated deliberateness and detachment that he brings to the course. But without the game, the effect is the opposite. Woods flows over a golf course as naturally as water finding its level. Off it, he can be wary and chilly.

Like so many other aspects of his life, the important decisions about how Woods will be spending his time at Stanford—and he insists he will stay the full four years—were carefully plotted long in advance.

His college plans calls for putting on some muscle and learning enough about accounting to monitor the people who will be watching the millions he will make in endorsement contracts the instant he turns pro. He doesn't have an agent yet, but the International Management Group, the sports marketing giant, had Earl Woods on its payroll as a consultant for several years.

Although an excellent student who graduated from public high school with a 3.79 grade-point average, Tiger shows little enthusiasm for anything he's been studying. He describes his Western civilization reading as "antiquity, stuff no one is ever going to need to know."

When Earl Woods sent his son off to France in September to compete in the World Amateur Championships in Versailles, he urged him "to smell the flowers and soak it all in." Tiger ate at McDonald's every night.

"I'm very blah," Tiger says. "It bothers my girlfriend sometimes, but that's just the way it is." (The only things Woods would reveal about his girlfriend is that she is from his hometown and not particularly interested in golf.) When I ask his parents how they would react if their son came home sporting an earring, like his teammate Begay, Tida and Earl shake their heads as if I just don't get it. "Tiger very very conservative," Tida says.

At Stanford, Woods's narrow agenda does not call for getting too close to his teammates, four of whom are returning starters from last year's national championship team with their own legitimate pro ambitions. The day before I arrived in Palo Alto, Woods had skipped practice, and Wally Goodwin, Stanford's Reaganesque head coach, tells me that the players had asked him "to bend Tiger's ear about it." Woods calls the lapse a "miscommunication."

His teammates say they have no problem being overshadowed by a freshman. (Woods won two of the four collegiate tournaments he competed in this fall while posting the second-lowest scoring average in the country.) What hurts is that Woods shows no interest in befriending them. When asked what Woods is like as a peron, they say they have no idea. Even Begay, who competed against Woods on the junior circuit, and says he has always felt an unspoken bond with him, says, "There's Tiger, and then there's the four of us."

Although his teammates hope a genuine relationship will develop, it's not likely to happen anytime soon. Asked to what extent a game like golf can ever be a team sport,

Woods says: "It's a team sport in that you're competing for a team as well as an individual title. I don't know what the other guys are doing, but I'm competing for both."

It's not that Woods can't be a generous teammate. He freely offers swing and putting tips to anyone with the good sense to seek his advice. It's just that Woods, following a script that was laid out before he was born, has other things to worry about besides getting touchy-feely with four college golfers. And what comes through so forcefully when you sit down with Woods is that he is not going to be easily shoved off course by anyone, whether it's his teammates, his coach, the press, a mugger, Hall Thompson or even the frequently excessive enthusiasms of his beloved old man.

"I'm the one who is sort of creating all this," Woods says. "And I'm the one who has to handle it."

New York Times Magazine, February 5, 1995

CHALLENGING
THE CATEGORIES

Ellen Goodman

He arrived at the Masters Tournament with all sorts of monikers, statistics and expectations added to his name. Eldrick Woods was "Tiger," the golf "phenom," the prodigy, the amateur champion playing for his first time with the pros.

The 19-year-old from Stanford University was also, the sports writers all calculated, the fourth black to play the whitebread golf event in 20 years, the first in seven years. He was compared to Jackie Robinson, Willie Mays, Michael Jordan.

But before Tiger Woods had left Augusta, Ga., in time to make a 9 a.m. Monday history class, he had firmly and repeatedly parsed his identity in his own way. He was not the designated black hope of a white sport.

"My mother is from Thailand," he said. "My father is part black, Chinese and American Indian. So I'm all of those. It's an injustice to all my heritages to single me out as black."

These were not the words of a young man trying to "pass," to deny his heritage, to reject the shade of melanin that would have categorized him as "Negro" under not-so-ancient race laws. This was a voice from a new generation of Americans who resist the cultural pressure to make one choice, who say I am the sum and the son of many parts.

For too long, slavery and racism have left a legacy in America that author Shirlee Taylor Haizlip calls either "an anxiety about authenticity or a paranoia about purity."

We look at the diffuse range of skin tones, hair types, eyes, noses, lips and try to force them into a handful of allotted races. More often than not we ask of some subtle shading, some "exotic" feature: "What is he?" "What is she?" Not who, mind you, but what.

Today our country may be more of a genetic melting pot than at any time in history. Yet we are often and oppositely as obsessed with ethnic and racial categories as any 19th-century census taker counting "octoroons" for his county.

Racism has been the natural enemy of a multiracial reality. It insisted that one drop of "African blood" made a white man black, although a drop of "white blood" didn't make him white. It accused a light-skinned woman if she tried to "pass" as white, though no one accused her of trying to pass as black.

To this day, there are blacks as well as whites as well as Asians as well as Hispanics who uphold this code, insisting that college freshmen "choose" which lunch table they will sit at, which sorority they will join. Children of diverse backgrounds are asked to choose sides as if race were a team.

Multiracial children can be caught in a kind of cultural cross fire. But increasingly, they are also the ones helping to create a demilitarized zone, trying to forge a bridge out of their own life experiences.

Finally, we've begun to hear the stories. In "Life on the Color Line," Gregory Williams has written a memoir of his childhood, "the true story of a white boy who discovered he was black." In "The Sweeter the Juice," Shirlee Haizlip has written about her search for and discovery of kin who "passed" into the white world, disappearing, leaving her own mother bewildered and abandoned.

Such stories reflect the pain created in American lives by color lines. But they also call into question the meaning and meaninglessness of race as a concept.

As Haizlip writes after her own search, "Genes and chromosomes from Africa, Europe and a pristine America commingled and created me. . . . I am an American anomaly. I am an American ideal. I am the American nightmare. I am the Martin Luther King dream. I am the new America."

The voices of these new Americans include many the age of Haizlip's children who have increasingly turned from pain to pride, less torn by racial heritages and more comfortable in two or three or four worlds. It's the Irish-Italian-Russian-American. It's the African-Asian-European-American.

These are the people who check "other" among the rigid categories offered by the census. They are the people who lobby for a "multiracial" slot, or no racial slot at all, on all the questionnaires that demand identity checks.

For their own sake, they struggle against the pressure to pick one of the mothers, fathers, grandparents on their family trees. And in that struggle they become a natural force against the divisions of race.

One of these new Americans is 19-year-old Tiger Woods, who says matter-of-factly, "All I can do is be myself." One-quarter black, one-quarter Thai, one-quarter Chinese, one-eighth American Indian and one-eighth white, his greatest natural asset is still the astounding ability to hit a golf ball 340 yards.

Boston Globe, April 13, 1995

FIVE ABOVE PAR

Ron Fimrite

The Stanford men's golf team has four All-Americans and a freshman who is, according to his coach, "potentially the greatest golfer who ever lived." Moreover, in the white-bread world of golf, this talented team is a veritable five-man Rainbow Coalition, a Cardinal-clad Benetton ad.

The conquering hero had come home. Well, Tiger Woods didn't exactly *conquer* the Masters at Augusta, Ga., finishing at five-over-par 293 in his first try at the legendary tournament, but he did exhibit enough of his prodigious talent to awe the galleries. He played even par for three of the four rounds and had the longest drives—averaging 311.1 yards on the holes where measurements were kept— of any of the contestants, outslugging even the

Bunyanesque John Daly. The trouble was, as his caddie, Tommy Bennett, observed, "He hit everything long," including approach shots and putts. "There ain't enough golf course out there for him."

But Woods, youngest of all U.S. Amateur champions, is already the stuff of which golfing dreams are made, and he remains a hero to his teammates on the defending NCAA champion Stanford golf team. So when he strode into the Cardinal clubhouse on the Monday morning after the Masters, he was hailed as a conqueror. "Tiger ... Tiger ... Tiger," they chorused. Then the razzing started. "Tiger, you never smiled once back there," chided Sara Hallock, a former golfer on the Cardinal women's team and now an administrative assistant for the men's team. "You looked so glum." Woods was abashed. "I never smile when I'm playing," he riposted. "I'm focused."

Now, of course, it's time to focus on defending that NCAA title. Woods, a 19-year-old freshman, wasn't even on the Farm when his teammates—William Yanagisawa, Notah Begay III, Casey Martin and Steve Burdick, along with Brad Lanning, who has since graduated—took the championship a year ago at the Stonebridge Country Club in McKinney, Tex. It was Stanford's first NCAA golf title in 41 years, and the pressure is most assuredly on to repeat, particularly with Tiger in tow.

"It's a completely different world with Tiger," says Burdick. "We're the favorites every time we go out there. It's added even more pressure, but it's been a good experience."

The Cardinals have learned that, even with Woods, they have to do more than show up, brandish their drivers and wait for the competition to run. Through the end of April, Stanford had played in 12 tournaments, winning five and finishing second in three others.

This team, says coach Wally Goodwin, "has a chance to make collegiate golfing history. We have three fifth-year seniors [Begay, Yanagisawa and Martin] and a fourth-year senior [Burdick]—all of them All-Americans. And then we have potentially the greatest golfer who ever lived. This is just a great team."

It is much more than that for, in the white-bread world of golf, collegiate or otherwise, this Cardinal team represents an ethnic and philosophical mix rarely found outside the corridors of the United Nations headquarters. Begay is Native American—half Pueblo, half Navajo. Yanagisawa is the son of Japanese immigrants. Woods is considered black, but he is actually only one-quarter African American, the rest of him being a bouillabaisse of Chinese, Thai, American Indian and Caucasian blood. When asked to indicate his ethnic origin, Woods invariably says Asian, in deference to his Bangkok-born mother, Kultida. His father, Earl, who is half black and part white, Asian and American Indian, is keenly aware that in this country one drop of African American blood is enough to identify a person as black. And so, Tiger Woods, at 18, necessarily became the first black U.S. Amateur champion last year and this past April only the fourth black ever to play in the Masters.

Woods simply thinks of himself as an American golfer, dismissing race as irrelevant. Begay, however, is so intensely proud of his heritage that he plasters his cheeks with clay, tribal style, before every tournament.

Martin and Burdick are active leaders of the Stanford chapter of Athletes in Action, a Christian Bible-study group, and Yanagisawa, the son of Buddhists, is a Christian convert and AIA member. Begay was raised as a Catholic, a part of his heritage dating, he says, "from the enslavement by the Spanish invaders of the Pueblo people."

"We enjoy being different," says Martin. "The average college team is country-club bred. We are unique."

Martin suffers from a congenital affliction—Klippel-Trenaunay-Weber syndrome—that inhibits the circulation in his right leg, withering it to half the circumference of his left. Without a full-length protective stocking, the leg swells painfully to an enormous size. Martin truly plays in pain, often excruciating pain. He will walk a course as long as he is physically able, then, by special NCAA dispensation, ride a cart between holes. Yet, he was named a second-team All-America selection last year by the U.S. Golf Coaches Association and, after an atypical opening round of 80 in the NCAA tournament, finished at 70–68–72. Like all of his teammates, he plans to play professionally.

Presiding over this disparate bunch is Goodwin, a cheerful if occasionally harassed 68-year-old, whose coaching career, in virtually every sport imaginable, spans some four decades. Goodwin was first exposed to life on the Stanford campus in 1952, a year after his graduation from the University of Virginia. Employed as a national officer of his college fraternity, Chi Psi, he was on an official "visit" to the Stanford chapter and enjoying a few beers with the brothers at Rossotti's when a noisy heckler disrupted the bonhomie. Goodwin's Eastern college attire—tweed coat, gray flannel slacks, white bucks—appeared to be the cause of this churlish fellow's indignation. Stanford *haute couture* of the time dictated white shirt, khaki pants and battered loafers.

Goodwin at first ignored the insults, but when the attack shifted to his rather prominent nose, he took understandable exception and dumped a mug of beer on the heckler's blond head. It was then that he learned his adversary had been none other than Gary Crosby, son of the famous actor-crooner, Bing.

Goodwin returned to Northern California in 1968, having occupied himself in the intervening years with attending to the family ranch in Wyoming, playing as an amateur on the Professional Golf Association circuit and coaching football, basketball, baseball and track at high schools in Colorado and Ohio. In 1968 he accepted a job as athletic director and coach of basketball and golf at Robert Louis Stevenson High School near Carmel. He stayed 10 years before moving on as an assistant basketball coach at Stetson University in De Land, Fla. After three years there, he became the golf coach at Northwestern University under athletic director Doug Single, a former Stanford football and rugby player. It was Single who recommended Goodwin to Cardinal athletic director Andy Geiger eight years ago. Goodwin was 60 when Geiger hired him, but he had lost none of his youthful pizzazz; within five years, he had produced a Pac–10 champion and his first All-American, Christian Cevaer, a French exchange student who had prepped at . . . where else? . . . Robert Louis Stevenson High School.

Next came Begay and Martin, then Burdick, then Yanagisawa, who transferred as a junior from the University of California–Irvine, and finally, the supreme catch, Tiger Woods from Cypress, Calif. Goodwin had had a headstart in the recruiting battle for Woods. When Woods was in the *seventh grade*, Goodwin had written him a letter expressing interest in having such a talented student and golfer come to Stanford. Goodwin's somewhat overzealous interest was understandable. At that point, Woods had already been in the public eye for 10 years—as a 3-year-old, he had beaten Bob Hope in a putting contest on national television.

When recruiting began in earnest, Goodwin's easygoing manner apparently charmed Woods' father, Earl, who, quite possibly, intimidated less intrepid recruiting rivals. "But from the first home visit," says Goodwin, "Earl and I were like peas in a pod." And not once has the elder Woods interfered with Goodwin's coaching or, for that matter, even visited his son on campus, an amazing show of restraint from one who lives but an hour's flight away and who had trained his son from diaperhood on to become a golf champion. Not that Goodwin's coaching technique is in any way comparable to Vince Lombardi's. "If I need to instruct a player," he says, "I've recruited the wrong guy. I coach 'teamness,' tempo and course knowledge. I tell them that today should never be considered perfect, that we're always getting ready for tomorrow. I love these kids so much I spoil them, but they haven't taken advantage of me yet."

Goodwin recruited Begay—whose second round 62 in last year's NCAA tournament set a course record and was the lowest score in the championship round history—without ever seeing him play golf. He did, however, watch him lead his Albuquerque Academy basketball team to the New Mexico state championship as a shooting guard. "I could see he was a great leader and a fierce competitor," Goodwin says.

Begay, who has a lively sense of humor, is one proud 22-year-old. The clay he places under his eyes before a match is there, he says, "because it is of the earth. It is a way of saying that though I'm facing a challenge, golf is not the be-all and end-all of my life, that there's more to me than this game."

Begay started playing golf regularly only because he needed something to do in the summers and baseball didn't appeal to him. Basketball and soccer were his games, but he was such a superior athlete that his golf kept pace with other sports, even though he didn't take it very seriously at first. By the time he had reached the Albuquerque Academy in the sixth grade—the first Native American admitted there—he was approaching championship caliber. John Fields, golf coach at the University of New Mexico, generously recommended him to Goodwin, knowing that Begay was eager to live elsewhere and was as ambitious academically as athletically.

Begay, Martin and Yanagisawa chose not to compete during their junior years. (The NCAA allows athletes to "redshirt" a year, sitting out for, say, an injury or an academic need, and to use the year of competitive eligibility later.) Martin says the three golfers had two goals in mind: "to get the bulk of schoolwork out of the way so we'd have more time for golf in our last year and—a vague and distant thought—to be there when Tiger Woods came to Stanford." The plan worked to perfection, says Martin, "because we extended the college experience, won a national championship and got Tiger." Begay's future plans are clearcut: He will play as an amateur this summer, try to make the U.S. Walker Cut team for a biennial competition against amateurs from Great Britain and Ireland in September and then turn professional. A degree in economics shouldn't hurt that future.

Martin, who will also receive a degree in economics later this month, has similar aspirations, but with some obvious reservations. "I want to play professionally," he says, "and if I can do it, I'll give it a try. I think my leg will hold up." There is no known cure for his circulatory disorder. "I just have to deal with it," he says. "When I'm swinging well, the leg seems fine. And yet it is there in my subconscious, and when I'm not playing well, the thought is always there that it could be the leg."

Martin grew up in a golfing family in Eugene, Ore. His older brother, Cameron, played at both UNLV and the University of Oregon. Though Martin is a "Duck fan for life," he felt the need to "get away" after playing on two state championship teams at South Eugene High. He committed himself to the Christian life in his sophomore year at Stanford. "It was not like God spoke to me from a burning bush or anything," he says. "I just felt I needed to live it as well as believe in it."

His faith is shared by Burdick, whom Martin introduced to Athletes in Action. Burdick needed no burning bush either. "I committed strongly to Christ my junior year in high school," he says. That's also about when he started playing golf seriously. Burdick grew up in Rocklin, north of Sacramento, and began playing at age 12 (Woods started before he was 2) at the Sunset Whitney Country Club. He may have started comparatively late, but he has, according to Goodwin, "the perfect temperament for the game. You never know what's going on inside him." Burdick became the star of the Stanford team in 1993, the year the three juniors redshirted, and was named a third-team All-American. "By sitting out a year, they gave me a chance to come out on my own, and I guess I did," he says.

Redshirting was more of a necessity than part of a calculated master plan for Yanagisawa, whose final round 64 in last year's NCAA tournament clinched the championship for Stanford. As a midterm transfer student, he had such a difficult time adjusting to the pressures of a new school that he lapsed for a time into clinical depression. He went home to Long Beach for the summer of '93 and "did some serious thinking. I knew I had to make a connection with this school. I'm at my best when there is a balance in my life, a balance between academics and athletics, a balance in all things."

He returned to Stanford in the fall of 1993 with a new determination, and he became, says Goodwin, the team's "little bulldog, a player whose last round is invariably his best." Off the course, Martin and Burdick, his roommate, involved him in AIA, and, newly balanced, he improved his grades dramatically in a psychology major. He graduates this month. "Casey and Steve have definitely helped me grow," Yanagisawa says. "We have representatives from every group on this team, and it's our diversity that helps us come together. In a tournament, we pull energy off each other. This has been an enriching experience for me."

Eldrick "Tiger" Woods relaxes with a hamburger outside the Stanford Golf Course clubhouse. He left Atlanta after the Masters at 9:12 p.m. and arrived at San Francisco International Airport at 1:20 a.m. It was well after 2 before he got to bed, and he had a history class, which he made, at 9 a.m. Despite the extraordinary attention paid this phenom, a player whom Stanford alumnus Tom Watson described as "potentially the most important to enter the game in 50 years," Woods says he had a "wonderful time" in Augusta. "I found out my game is good enough to compete at that level, but that there's a huge difference between competing and winning. I learned my game needs refinement, particularly in distance control. The pros are so precise with their shots."

It is 1 in the afternoon, and Woods, who has had little sleep, nevertheless looks fresh. At something over six feet tall—he's listed at 6'2" but seems a shade shorter—and with his weight up near 160 pounds, he has acquired some needed heft, though he still looks positively fragile and his facial features seem surprisingly delicate. There is, however, an inner toughness to this youngster and, after years in the limelight already, a rare maturity. But he's still a freshman, and he knows it.

"I had a tougher time with academics because I started playing golf as soon as I entered school," he notes. "If, say, I'd redshirted, it would have been a different story. As it is, it took me a full quarter to get adjusted. And this was the first time I'd been away from home. It was my dad's decision to stay away. He didn't want to interfere with my college experience, but if I ever need him, he'll come up. I talk to my family once or twice a week, anyway." He pauses to take a meaningful bite from the burger. "I know I've grown a lot since I've been here—my father says the same thing. We both agree there's been a tremendous difference in me this past year."

And Stanford? Does he like it? He laughs as if to say, "Are you kidding?" then gestures grandly at the flowing expanse of green fairways and at the rolling and blue forested hills beyond.

"Why, just look at all this," he says, smiling proprietarily. "It's beautiful. Really beautiful."

Stanford Alumni magazine, June 1995

A DISHONEST
AD CAMPAIGN

James K. Glassman

You don't have to like golf to love Tiger Woods. His swing is a triumph of poetry over physics, sending drives 350 yards down the fairway. And, like the very best golfers—Jones, Hogan, Nicklaus—he converts passion and concentration into a kind of spirituality.

After winning three U.S. Amateur titles in a row, Woods turned professional last month, signing endorsement contracts with Nike and Titleist that are worth $60 million over five years. He's played well, too, nearly winning a tournament in Illinois.

Three other things to love about Tiger Woods: He's young (just 20), smart (a junior at Stanford) and black.

That last characteristic is particularly unusual. Only 3.6 percent of the 25 millions golfers in this country are African American. And black professional golfers—like Jewish skeet-shooters, Hispanic hockey players and Italian American hurdlers—are rare.

Woods is so good and, as a young black person (I should note here that in fact his father is African American, his mother of Thai extraction) playing golf, so unusual, that nearly everyone is cheering for him. That's why the advertising campaign that Nike has mounted for Woods is so discordant, dishonest and even vile.

The modest Tiger Woods may be the darling of duffers—white and black—and of the entire press corps, but Nike has decided that the best way to sell shoes is to portray him as a defiant victim of American racism.

On Aug. 29, Woods made his pro debut in a three-page Nike ad in the Wall Street Journal. The ad depicted a cocky Woods ticking off his achievements ("I shot in the 60s when I was 12," etc.) and saying, "There are still courses in the United States that I am not allowed to play because of the color of my skin."

This is utter nonsense. Perhaps in the past, Woods was denied invitations to private country clubs. But that's not what the ad said. It claimed that today, Tiger Woods, easily one of the half-dozen most popular golfers in the world, can't play where he wants.

The ad is telling blacks and other minorities that racism is so virulent in this country that, no matter how good you are, you will be despised and rejected by whites. You have to stand up to them (in Nikes, of course).

The ad concludes with Woods saying, "I've heard I'm not ready for you. Are you ready for me?" This is just the sort of hip, hoops-in-the-hood image that Nike has carefully cultivated to appeal not just to minorities but to with-it whites.

The only problem is that, in the case of Woods, it's based on a lie. I called Nike to get a list of the courses he's not allowed to play. Finally, James Small, the company's public relations director in Beaverton, Ore., called me back.

"You're absolutely right," he admitted, affably. "Tiger Woods can play on any golf course he wants."

In other words, the ad campaign's entire premise is wrong?

Well, not exactly, said Small. "The goal of the ad was to raise awareness that golf is not an inclusive sport."

It's true that a lot of courses are private clubs, and clubs by definition are not "inclusive." But most courses—including great ones like Pebble Beach—are open to the public.

No, the average golfer (black or white) can't get a starting time at the exclusive Chevy Chase Club. But, certainly Tiger Woods can. And the reason he transcends the normal restrictions of private clubs is that he is a terrific golfer.

In this country, merit trumps race. That fact is one of the glories of our market republic. If you're good enough, people will buy what you're selling no matter who you are.

After all, the most popular entertainer in America, in terms of earnings, is a black woman named Oprah Winfrey (she netted $97 million last year, says Forbes). The most popular sports figure, Michael Jordan, is also black. So is the most popular politician, Colin Powell.

In fact, Woods is making his $60 million in large part *because* he is black. Whites, too, love an underdog and a rarity.

Are African Americans denied opportunities because of their skin color? Yes. The sad truth is that racial, ethnic and religious prejudices will endure in this country, as they have in every other.

But why exaggerate? In the case of Nike, an $8 billion company that just reported record profits yesterday, the shameful answer seems to be money. It's not hard to understand. Myths of racism and victimization sell big. Just look at rap music.

Nike knows that the best way to sell undifferentiated products is by endowing them with an aura or an attitude. A favorite attitude among advertisers today is cheek. Apple Computer, Seven-Up and Benetton have used this posture well, but it's getting hackneyed. Even Amtrak is running an ad that features a huge photo of coy blonde and the copy:

"'She's reading Nietzsche,' Harris noted to himself as he walked towards the cafe car for a glass of cabernet. And as he passed her seat, Maureen looked up from her book and thought, 'Nice buns.'"

It's good to see Nike reaching beyond this banality—but what's wrong with responsibility and honesty?

Nike is also smart to recognize a huge untapped market for golf shoes and clothes—and smart to see Woods as the ticket to it. "He's going to bring minorities to the game and youth to the game," says Merle Marting of Nike's golf division.

I have my doubts about whether a bucolic five-hour round of golf will ever appeal to the young and the restless, but I hope Nike is right. Stuffy duffers in lime-green pants have dominated the greens too long.

Tiger Woods may be just the guy to change things—not by being portrayed as a phony victim but by being celebrated as a master of a very difficult, very beautiful game.

Washington Post, September 17, 1996

THE CHOSEN ONE

Gary Smith

It was ordinary. It was oh so ordinary. It was a salad, a dinner roll, a steak, a half potato, a slice of cake, a clinking fork, a podium joke, a ballroom full of white-linen-tablecloth conversation. Then a thick man with tufts of white hair rose from the head table. His voice trembled and his eyes teared and his throat gulped down sobs between words, and everything ordinary was cast out of the room.

He said, "Please forgive me. . .but sometimes I get very emotional. . .when I talk about my son. . . .My heart. . .fills with so. . . much. . .joy. . .when I realize. . .that this young man. . .is going to be able. . .to help so many people. . . . He will transcend this game. . .and bring to the world. . .a humanitarianism. . .which has never been known before.

The world will be a better place to live in. . .by virtue of his existence. . .and his presence. . . . I acknowledge only a small part in that. . .in that I know that I was personally selected by God himself. . .to nurture this young man. . .and bring him to the point where he can make his contribution to humanity. . . . This is my treasure. . . . Please accept it. . .and use it wisely. . . . Thank you."

Blinking tears, the man found himself inside the arms of his son and the applause of the people, all up on their feet.

In the history of American celebrity, no father has ever spoken this way. Too many dads have deserted or died before their offspring reached this realm, but mostly they have fallen mute, the father's vision exceeded by the child's, leaving the child to wander, lost, through the sad and silly wilderness of modern fame.

So let us stand amidst this audience at last month's Fred Haskins Award dinner to honor America's outstanding college golfer of 1996, and take note as Tiger and Earl Woods embrace, for a new manner of celebrity is taking form before our eyes. Regard the 64-year-old African-American father, arm upon the superstar's shoulder, right where the chip is so often found, declaring that this boy will do more good for the world than any man who ever walked it. Gaze at the 20-year-old son, with the blood of four races in his veins, not flinching an inch from the yoke of his father's prophecy but already beginning to scent the complications. The son who stormed from behind to win a record third straight U.S. Amateur last

August, turned pro and rang up scores in the 60s in 21 of his first 27 rounds, winning two PGA Tour events as he doubled and tripled the usual crowds and dramatically changed their look and age.

Now turn. Turn and look at us, the audience, standing in anticipation of something different, something pure. Quiet. Just below the applause, or within it, can you hear the grinding? That's the relentless chewing mechanism of fame, girding to grind the purity and the promise to dust. Not the promise of talent, but the bigger promise, the father's promise, the one that stakes everything on the boy's not becoming separated from his own humanity and from all the humanity crowding around him.

It's a fitting moment, while he's up there at the head table with the audience on its feet, to anoint Eldrick (Tiger) Woods—the rare athlete to establish himself immediately as the dominant figure in his sport—as *Sports Illustrated*'s 1996 Sportsman of the Year. And to pose a question: Who will win? The machine. . . or the youth who has just entered its maw?

Tiger Woods will win. He'll fulfill his father's vision because of his mind, one that grows more still, more willful, more efficient, the greater the pressure upon him grows.

The machine will win because it has no mind. It flattens even as it lifts, trivializes even as it exalts, spreads a man so wide and thin that he becomes margarine soon enough.

Tiger will win because of God's mind. Can't you see the pattern? Earl Woods asks. Can't you see the signs? "Tiger will do more than any other man in history to change the course of humanity," Earl says.

Sports history, Mr. Woods? Do you mean more than Joe Louis and Jackie Robinson, more than Muhammad Ali and Arthur Ashe? "More than any of them because he's more charismatic, more educated, more prepared for this than anyone."

Anyone, Mr. Woods? Your son will have more impact than Nelson Mandela, more than Gandhi, more than Buddha?

"Yes, because he has a larger forum than any of them. Because he's playing a sport that's international. Because he's qualified through his ethnicity to accomplish miracles. He's the bridge between the East and the West. There is no limit because he has the guidance. I don't know yet exactly what form this will take. But he is the Chosen One. He'll have the power to impact nations. Not people. Nations. The world is just getting a taste of his power."

Surely this is lunacy. Or are we just too myopic to see? One thing is certain: We are witnessing the first volley of an epic encounter, the machine at its mightiest confronting the individual groomed all his life to conquer it and turn it to his use. The youth who has been exposed to its power since he toddled onto The *Mike Douglas Show* at three, the set of *That's Incredible!* at five, the boy who has been steeled against the silky seduction to which so many before him have succumbed. The one who, by all appearances, brings more psychological balance, more sense of self, more consciousness of possibility to the battlefield than any of his predecessors.

This is war, so let's start with war. Remove the images of pretty putting greens from the movie screen standing near the ballroom's head table. Jungle is what's needed here, foliage up to a man's armpits, sweat trickling down his thighs, leeches crawling up them. Lieut. Col. Earl Woods, moving through the night with his rifle ready, wondering why a U.S. Army public information officer stationed in Brooklyn decided in his mid–30s that he belonged in the Green Berets and ended up doing two tours of duty in Vietnam. Wondering why his first marriage has died and why the three children from it have ended up without a dad around when it's dark like this and it's time for bed—just as Earl ended up as a boy after his own father died. Wondering why he keeps plotting ways to return to the line of fire—"creative soldiering," he calls it—to eyeball death once more. To learn once again about his dark and cold side, the side that enables Earl, as Tiger will remark years later, "to slit your throat and then sit down and eat his dinner."

Oh, yes, Earl is one hell of a cocktail. A little Chinese, a little Cherokee, a few shots of African-American; don't get finicky about measurements, we're making a vat here. Pour in some gruffness and a little intimidation, then some tenderness and some warmth and a few jiggers of old anger. Don't hold back on intelligence. And stoicism. Add lots of stoicism, and even more of responsibility—"the most responsible son of a bitch you've ever seen in your life" is how Earl himself puts it. Top it all with "a bucket of whiskey," which is what he has been known to order when he saunters into a bar and he's in the mood. Add a dash of hyperbole, maybe two, and to hell with the ice, just whir. This is one of those concoctions you're going to remember when morning comes.

Somewhere in there, until a good 15 years ago, there was one other ingredient, the existential Tabasco, the smoldering why? The Thai secretary in the U.S. Army office in Bangkok smelled it soon after she met Earl, in 1967. "He couldn't relax," says Kultida (Tida) Woods. "Searching for something, always searching, never satisfied. I think because both his parents died when he was young, and he didn't have Mom and Dad to make him warm. Sometimes he stayed awake till three or four in the morning, just thinking."

In a man so accustomed to exuding command and control, in a Green Beret lieutenant colonel, why? has a way of building up power like a river dammed. Why did the Vietcong sniper bracket him that day (first bullet a few inches left of one ear, second bullet a few inches right of the other) but never fire the third bullet? Why did Earl's South Vietnamese combat buddy, Nguyen Phong—the one Earl nicknamed Tiger, and in whose memory he would nickname his son—stir one night just in time to awaken Earl and warn him not to budge because a viper was poised inches from his right eye? What about that road Earl's jeep rolled down one night, the same road on which two friends had just been mutilated, the road that took him through a village so silent and dark that his scalp tingled, and then, just beyond it. . . hell turned inside-out over his shoulder, the sky lighting up and all the huts he had just passed spewing Vietcong machine-gun and artillery fire? He never understands what is the purpose of Lieutenant Colonel Woods's surviving again and again. He never quite comprehends what is the point of his life, until. . . .

Until the boy is born. He will get all the time that Earl was unable to devote to the three children from his first marriage. He will be the only child from Earl's second marriage, to the Thai woman he brought back to America, and right away there are signs. What other six-month-old, Earl asks, has the balance to stand in the palm of his father's hand and remain there even as Daddy strolls around the house? Was there another 11-month-old, ever, who could pick up a sawed-off club, imitate his father's golf swing so fluidly and drive the ball so wickedly into the nylon net across the garage? Another four-year-old who could be dropped off at the golf course at 9 a.m. on a Saturday and picked up at 5 p.m., pockets bulging with money he had won from disbelievers 10 and 20 years older, until Pop said, "Tiger, you can't do that"? Earl starts to get a glimmer. He is to be the father of the world's most gifted golfer.

But why? What for? Not long after Tiger's birth, when Earl has left the military to become a purchaser for McDonnell Douglas, he finds himself in a long discussion with a woman he knows. She senses the power pooling inside him, the friction. "You have so much to give," she tells him, "but you're not giving it. You haven't even scratched the surface of your potential." She suggests he try est, Erhard Seminars Training, an intensive self-discovery and self-actualizing technique, and it hits Earl hard, direct mortar fire to the heart. What he learns is that his overmuscular sense of responsibility for others has choked his potential.

"To the point," says Earl, "that I wouldn't even buy a handkerchief for myself. It went all the way back to the day my father died, when I was 11, and my mother put her arm around me after the funeral and said, 'You're the man of the house now.' I became the father that young, looking out for everyone else, and then she died two years later.

"What I learned through est was that by doing more for myself, I could do much more for others. Yes, be responsible, but love life, and give people the space to be in your life, and allow yourself room to give to others. That caring and sharing is what's most important, not being responsible for everyone else. Which is where Tiger comes in. What I learned led me to give so much time to Tiger, and to give him the space to be himself, and not to smother him with dos and don'ts. I took out the authority aspect and turned it into companionship. I made myself vulnerable as a parent. When you have to earn respect from your child, rather than demanding it because it's owed to you as the father, miracles happen. I realized that, through him, the giving could take a quantum leap. What I could do on a limited scale, he could do on a global scale."

At last, the river is undammed, and Earl's whole life makes sense. At last, he sees what he was searching for, a pattern. No more volunteering for missions—he has his. Not simply to be a great golfer's father. To be destiny's father. His son will change the world.

"What the hell had I been doing in public information in the Army, posted in Brooklyn?" he asks. "Why, of course, what greater training can there be than three years of dealing with the New York media to prepare me to teach Tiger the importance of public relations and how to handle the media?"

Father: Where were you born, Tiger?

Son, age three: I was born on December 30, 1975, in Long Beach, California.

Father: No, Tiger, only answer the question you were asked. It's important to prepare yourself for this. Try again.

Son: I was born in Long Beach, California.

Father: Good, Tiger, good.

The late leap into the Green Berets? "What the hell was that for?" Earl says. "Of course, to prepare me to teach Tiger mental toughness."

The three children by the first marriage? "Not just one boy the first time," says Earl, "but two, along with a girl, as if God was saying, 'I want this son of a bitch to really have previous training.'"

The Buddhist wife, the one who grew up in a boarding school after her parents separated when she was five, the girl who then vowed that her child would know nothing but love and attention? The one who will preach inner calm to Tiger simply by turning to him with that face—still awaiting its first wrinkle at 52? Whose eyes close when she speaks, so he can almost see her gathering and sifting the thoughts? The mother who will walk every hole and keep score for Tiger at children's tournaments, adding a stroke or two if his calm cracks? "Look at this stuff!" cries Earl. "Over and over you can see the plan being orchestrated by someone other than me because I'm not this damn good! I tried to get out of that combat assignment to Thailand. But Tida was meant to bring in the influence of the Orient, to introduce Tiger to Buddhism and inner peace, so he would have the best of two different worlds. And so he would have the knowledge that there were two people whose lives were totally committed to him."

What of the heart attack Earl suffered when Tiger was 10 and the retired lieutenant colonel felt himself floating down the gray tunnel toward the light before he was wrenched back? "To prepare me to teach Tiger that life is short," Earl says, "and to live each day to the maximum, and not worry about the future. There's only now. You must understand that time is just a linear measurement of successive increments of now. Anyplace you go on that line is now, and that's how you have to live it."

No need to wonder about the appearance of the perfect childhood coach, John Anselmo; the perfect sports psychologist, Jay Brunza; the perfect agent, Hughes Norton; the perfect attorney, John Merchant; and the perfect pro swing instructor, Butch Harmon. Or about the great tangle of fate that leads them all to Tiger at just the right junctures in his development. "Everything," says Earl, "right there when he needs it. Everything. There can't be this much coincidence in the world. This is a directed scenario, and none of us involved in the scenario has failed to accept the responsibility. This is all destined to be."

His wife ratifies this, in her own way. She takes the boy's astrological chart to a Buddhist temple in Los Angeles and to another in Bangkok and is told by monks at both places that the child has wondrous powers. "If he becomes a politician, he will be either a president or a prime minister," she is told. "If he enters the military, he will be a general."

Tida comes to a conclusion. "Tiger has Thai, African, Chinese, American Indian and European blood," she says. "He can hold everyone together. He is the Universal Child."

This is in the air the boy breathes for 20 years, and it becomes bone fact for him, marrow knowledge. When asked about it, he merely nods in acknowledgment of it, assents to it; of course he believes it's true. So failure, in the rare visits it pays him, is not failure. It's just life pausing to teach him a lesson he needs in order to go where he's inevitably going. And success, no matter how much sooner than expected it comes to the door, always finds him dressed and ready to welcome it. "Did you ever see yourself doing this so soon?" a commentator breathlessly asks him seconds after his first pro victory, on Oct. 6 in Las Vegas, trying to elicit wonder and awe on live TV. "Yeah," Tiger responds. "I kind of did." And sleep comes to him so easily: In the midst of conversation, in a car, in a plane, off he goes, into the slumber of the destined. "I don't see any of this as scary or a burden," Tiger says. "I see it as fortunate. I've always known where I wanted to go in life. I've never let anything deter me. This is my purpose. It will unfold."

No sports star in the history of American celebrity has spoken this way. Maybe, somehow, Tiger can win.

The machine will win. It must win because it too is destiny, five billion destinies leaning against one. There are ways to keep the hordes back, a media expert at Nike tells Tiger. Make broad gestures when you speak. Keep a club in your hands and take practice swings, or stand with one foot well out in front of the other, in almost a karate stance. That will give you room to breathe. Two weeks later, surrounded by a pen-wielding mob in La Quinta, Calif., in late November, just before the Skins Game, the instruction fails. Tiger survives, but his shirt and slacks are ruined, felt-tip-dotted to death.

The machine will win because it will wear the young man down, cloud his judgment, steal his sweetness, the way it does just before the Buick Challenge in Pine Mountain, Ga., at the end of September. It will make his eyes drop when the fans' gaze reaches for his, his voice growl at their clawing hands, his body sag onto a sofa after a practice round and then rise and walk across the room and suddenly stop in bewilderment. "I couldn't even remember what I'd just gotten off the couch for, two seconds before," he says. "I was like mashed potatoes. Total mush."

So he walks. Pulls out on the eve of the Buick Challenge, pulls out of the Fred Haskins Award dinner to honor him, and goes home. See, maybe Tiger can win. He can just turn his back on the machine and walk. Awards? Awards to Tiger are like echoes, voices bouncing off the walls, repeating what a truly confident man has already heard inside his own head. The Jack Nicklaus Award, the one Jack himself was supposed to present to Tiger live on ABC during the Memorial tournament last spring? Tiger would have blown it off if Wally Goodwin, his coach at Stanford during the two years he played there before turning pro, hadn't insisted that he show up.

The instant Tiger walks away from the Buick Challenge and the Haskins dinner, the hounds start yapping. See, that's why the machine will win. It's got all those damn heel-nippers. Little mutts on the PGA Tour resenting how swiftly the 20-year-old was ordained, how hastily he was invited to play practice rounds with Nicklaus and Arnold Palmer, with Greg Norman and Ray Floyd and Nick Faldo and Fred Couples. And big dogs snapping too. Tom Kite quoted as saying, "I can't ever remember being tired when I was 20," and Peter Jacobsen quoted, "You can't compare Tiger to Nicklaus and Palmer anymore because they never [walked out]."

He rests for a week, stunned by the criticism—"I thought those people were my friends," he says. He never second-guesses his decision to turn pro, but he sees what he surrendered. "I miss college," he says. "I miss hanging out with my friends, getting in a little trouble. I have to be so guarded now. I miss sitting around drinking beer and talking half the night. There's no one my own age to hang out with anymore because almost everyone my age is in college. I'm a target for everybody now, and there's nothing I can do about it. My mother was right when she said that turning pro would take away my youth. But golfwise, there was nothing left for me in college."

He reemerges after the week's rest and rushes from four shots off the lead on the final day to win the Las Vegas Invitational in sudden death. The world's waiting for him again, this time with reinforcements. Letterman and Leno want him as a guest; GQ calls about a cover; Cosby, along with almost every other sitcom you can think of, offers to write an episode revolving around Tiger, if only he'll appear. Kids dress up as Tiger for Halloween—did anyone ever dress up as Arnie or Jack?—and Michael Jordan declares that his only hero on earth is Tiger Woods. Pepsi is dying to have him cut a commercial for one of its soft drinks aimed at Generation Xers; Nike and Titleist call in chits for the $40 million and $20 million contracts he signed; money managers are eager to know how he wants his millions invested; women walk onto the course during a practice round and ask for his hand in marriage; kids stampede over and under ropes and chase him from the 18th hole to the clubhouse; piles of phone messages await him when he returns to his hotel room. "Why," Tiger asks, "do so many people want a piece of me?"

Because something deeper than conventional stardom is at work here, something so spontaneous and subconscious that words have trouble going there. It's a communal craving, a public aching for a superstar free of anger and arrogance and obsession with self. It's a hollow place that chimes each time Tiger and his parents strike the theme of father and mother and child love, each time Tiger stands at a press conference and declares, "They have raised me well, and I truly believe they have taught me to accept full responsibility for all aspects of my life." During the making of a Titleist commercial in November, a makeup woman is so moved listening to Earl describe his bond with Tiger that she decides to contact her long-estranged father. "See what I mean?" cries Earl. "Did you affect someone that way today? Did anyone else there? It's destiny, man. It's something bigger than me."

What makes it so vivid is context. The white canvas that the colors are being painted on—the moneyed, mature and almost minority-less world of golf—makes Tiger an emblem of youth overcoming age, have-not overcoming have, outsider overcoming insider, to the delight not only of the 18-year-olds in the gallery wearing nose rings and cornrows, but also—of all people—of the aging insider haves.

So Tiger finds himself, just a few weeks after turning pro at the end of August, trying to clutch a bolt of lightning with one hand and steer an all-at-once corporation—himself—with the other, and before this he has never worked a day in his life. Never mowed a neighbor's lawn, never flung a folded newspaper, never stocked a grocery shelf; Mozarts just don't, you know. And he has to act as if none of this is new or vexing because he has this characteristic—perhaps from all those years of hanging out with his dad at tournaments, all those years of mixing with and mauling golfers five, 10, 20, 30 years older than he is—of never permitting himself to appear confused, surprised or just generally a little squirt. "His favorite expression," Earl says, "is, 'I knew that.'" Of course Pop, who is just as irreverent with Tiger as he is reverent, can say, "No, you didn't know that, you little s–." But Earl, who has always been the filter for Tiger, decides to take a few steps back during his son's first few months as a pro because he wishes to encourage Tiger's independence and because he is uncertain of his own role now that the International Management Group (IMG) is managing Tiger's career.

Nobody notices it, but the inner calm is beginning to dissolve. Earl enters Tiger's hotel room during the Texas Open in mid-October to ask him about his schedule, and Tiger does something he has never done in his 20 years. He bites the old man's head off.

Earl blinks. "I understand how you must feel," he says.

"No, you don't," snaps Tiger.

"And I realized," Earl says later, "that I'd spent 20 years planning for this, but the one thing I didn't do was educate Tiger to be the boss of a corporation. There was just no vehicle for that, and I thought it would develop more slowly. I wasn't presumptuous enough to anticipate this. For the first time in his life, the training was behind the reality. I could see on his face that he was going through hell."

The kid is fluid, though. Just watch him walk. He's quick to flow into the new form, to fit the contour of necessity.

A few hours after the outburst he's apologizing to his father and hugging him. A few days later he's giving Pop the O.K. to call a meeting of the key members of Tiger's new corporation and establish a system, Lieutenant Colonel Woods in command, chairing a 2 1/2-hour teleconference with the team each week to sift through all the demands, weed out all the chaff and present Tiger five decisions to make instead of 500. A few days after that, the weight forklifted off his shoulders, at least temporarily, Tiger wins the Walt Disney World/Oldsmobile Classic. And a few weeks later, at the Fred Haskins Award dinner, which has been rescheduled at his request, Tiger stands at the podium and says, "I should've attended the dinner [the first time]. I admit I was wrong, and I'm sorry for any inconvenience I may have caused. But I have learned from that, and I will never make that mistake again. I'm very honored to be part of this select group, and I'll always remember, for both good and bad, this Haskins Award; for what I did and what I learned, for the company I'm now in and I'll always be in. Thank you very much." The crowd surges to its feet, cheering once more.

See, maybe Tiger can win. He's got the touch. He's got the feel. He never writes down a word before he gives a speech. When he needs to remember a phone number, he doesn't search his memory or a little black book; he picks up a phone and watches what number his fingers go to. When he needs a 120-yard shot to go under an oak branch and over a pond, he doesn't visualize the shot, as most golfers would. He looks at the flag and pulls everything from the hole back, back, back. . . not back into his mind's eye, but into his hands and forearms and hips, so they'll do it by feel. Explain how he made that preposterous shot? He can't. Better you interview his knuckles and metacarpals.

"His handicap," says Earl, "is that he has such a powerful creative mind. His imagination is too vivid. If he uses visualization, the ball goes nuts. So we piped into his creative side even deeper, into his incredible sense of feel."

"I've learned to trust the subconscious," says Tiger. "My instincts have never lied to me."

The mother radiates this: the Eastern proclivity to let life happen, rather than the Western one to make it happen. The father comes to it in his own way, through fire. To kill a man, to conduct oneself calmly and efficiently when one's own death is imminent—a skill Earl learns in Green Berets psychological training and then again and again in jungles and rice paddies—one removes the conscious mind from the task and yields to the subconscious. "It's the more powerful of the two minds," Earl says. "It works faster than the conscious mind, yet it's patterned enough to handle routine tasks over and over, like driving a car or making a putt. It knows what to do.

"Allow yourself the freedom of emotion and feeling. Don't try to control them and trap them. Acknowledge them and become the beneficiary of them. Let it all outflow."

Let it all because it's all there: The stability, almost freakish for a close-of-the-millennium California child—same two parents, same house all his 20 years, same best friends, one since second grade, one since eighth. The kid, for god's sake, never once had a babysitter. The conditioning is there as well, the two years of psychological boot camp during which Earl dropped golf bags and pumped cart brakes during Tiger's backswings, jingled change and rolled balls across his line of vision to test his nerves, promising him at the outset that he only had to say "Enough" and Earl would cut off the blowtorch, but promising too that if Tiger graduated, no man he ever faced would be mentally stronger than he. "I am the toughest golfer mentally," Tiger says.

The bedrock is so wide that opposites can dance upon it: The cautious man can be instinctive, the careful man can be carefree. The bedrock is so wide that it has enticed Tiger into the habit of falling behind—as he did in the final matches of all three U.S. Junior Amateur and all three U.S. Amateur victories—knowing in his tissue and bones that danger will unleash his greatest power. "Allow success and fame to happen," the old man says. "Let the legend grow."

To hell with the Tao. The machine will win, it has to win, because it makes everything happen before a man knows it. Before he knows it, a veil descends over his eyes when another stranger approaches. Before he knows it, he's living in a walled community with an electronic gate and a security guard, where the children trick-or-treat in golf carts, a place like the one Tiger just moved into in Orlando to preserve some scrap of sanity. Each day there, even with all the best intentions, how can he help but be a little more removed from the world he's supposed to change, and from his truest self?

Which is. . . who? The poised, polite, opaque sage we see on TV? No, no, no; his friends hoot and haze him when they see that Tiger on the screen, and he can barely help grinning himself. The Tiger they know is perfectly 20, a fast-food freak who never remembers to ask if anyone else is hungry before he bolts to Taco Bell or McDonald's for the 10th time of the week. The one who loves riding roller coasters, spinning out golf carts and winning at cards no matter how often his father accuses him of "reckless eye-balling." The one who loves delivering the dirty joke, who owns a salty barracks tongue just a rank or two beneath his father's. The one who's flip, who's downright cocky. When a suit walks up to him before the Haskins Award dinner and says, "I think you're going to be the next great one, but those are mighty big shoes to fill," Tiger replies, "Got big feet."

A typical exchange between Tiger and his agent, Norton:

"Tiger, they want to know when you can do that interview."

"Tell them to kiss my ass!"

"All right, and after that, what should I tell them?"

"Tell them to kiss my ass again!"

"O.K., and after that. . . ."

But it's a cockiness cut with humility, the paradox pounded into his skull by a father who in one breath speaks of his son with religious awe and in the next grunts, "You weren't s– then, Tiger. You ain't s– now. You ain't never gonna be s–."

"That's why I know I can handle all this," Tiger says, "no matter how big it gets. I grew up in the media's eye, but I was taught never to lose sight of where I came from. Athletes aren't as gentlemanly as they used to be. I don't like that change. I like the idea of being a role model. It's an honor. People took the time to help me as a kid, and they impacted my life. I want to do the same for kids."

So, if it's a clinic for children instead of an interview or an endorsement for adults, the cynic in Tiger gives way to the child who grew up immersed in his father's vision of an earth-altering compassion, the seven-year-old boy who watched scenes from the Ethiopian famine on the evening news, went right to his bedroom and returned with a $20 bill to contribute from his piggy bank. Last spring busloads of inner-city kids would arrive at golf courses where Tiger was playing for Stanford, spilling out to watch the Earl and Tiger show in wonder. Earl would talk about the dangers of drugs, then proclaim, "Here's Tiger Woods on drugs," and Tiger would stagger to the tee, topping the ball so it bounced crazily to the side. And then, presto, with a wave of his arms Earl would remove the drugs from Tiger's body, and his son would stride to the ball and launch a 330-yard rocket across the sky. Then Earl would talk about respect and trust and hard work and demonstrate what they can all lead to by standing 10 feet in front of his son, raising his

arms and telling Tiger to smash the ball between them—
and, whoosh, Tiger would part not only the old man's arms
but his haircut too.

They've got plans, the two of them, big plans, for a Tiger
Woods Foundation that will fund scholarships across the
country, set up clinics and coaches and access to golf
courses for inner-city children. "I throw those visions out
there in front of him," Earl says, "and it's like reeling in a
fish. He goes for the bait, takes it and away he goes. This is
nothing new. It's been working this way for a long time."

"That's the difference," says Merchant, Tiger's attorney
and a family friend. "Other athletes who have risen to this
level just didn't have this kind of guidance. With a father
and mother like Tiger's, he has to be real. It's such a rare
quality in celebrities nowadays. There hasn't been a politician since John Kennedy whom people have wanted to
touch. But watch Tiger. He has it. He actually listens to
people when they stop him in an airport. He looks them in
the eye. I can't ever envision Tiger Woods selling his auto-
graph."

See, maybe Tiger can win.

Let's be honest. The machine will win because you can't
work both sides of this street. The machine will win
because you can't transcend wearing 16 Nike swooshes, you
can't move human hearts while you're busy pushing sneak-
ers. Gandhi didn't hawk golf balls, did he? Jackie Robinson
was spared that fate because he came and went while Madi-
son Avenue was still teething. Ali became a symbol instead

of a logo because of boxing's disrepute and because of the attrition of cells in the basal ganglia of his brain. Who or what will save Tiger Woods?

Did someone say Buddha?

Every year near his birthday, Tiger goes with his mother to a Buddhist temple and makes a gift of rice, sugar and salt to the monks there who have renounced all material goods. A mother-of-pearl Buddha given to Tiger by his Thai grandfather watches over him while he sleeps, and a gold Buddha hangs from the chain on his neck. "I like Buddhism because it's a whole way of being and living," Tiger says. "It's based on discipline and respect and personal responsibility. I like Asian culture better than ours because of that. Asians are much more disciplined than we are. Look how well behaved their children are. It's how my mother raised me. You can question, but talk back? Never. In Thailand, once you've earned people's respect, you have it for life. Here it's, What have you done for me lately? So here you can never rest easy. In this country I have to be very careful. I'm easygoing, but I won't let you in completely. There, I'm Thai, and it feels very different. In many ways I consider that home.

"I believe in Buddhism. Not every aspect, but most of it. So I take bits and pieces. I don't believe that human beings can achieve ultimate enlightenment, because humans have flaws. I don't want to get rid of all my wants and desires. I can enjoy material things, but that doesn't mean I need them. It doesn't matter to me whether I live in a place like this"—the golf club in his hand makes a sweep of the Orlando villa—"or in a shack. I'd be fine in a shack, as long as I could play some golf. I'll do the commercials for Nike and for Titleist, but there won't be much more than that. I have no desire to be the king of endorsement money."

On the morning after he decides to turn pro, there's a knock on his hotel room door. It's Norton, bleary-eyed but exhilarated after a late-night round of negotiations with Nike. He explains to Tiger and Earl that the benchmark for contract endorsements in golf is Norman's reported $2 $\frac{1}{2}$ million-a-year deal with Reebok. Then, gulping down hard on the yabba-dabba-doo rising up his throat, Norton announces Nike's offer: $40 million for five years, eight mil a year. "Over three times what Norman gets!" Norton exults.

Silence.

"Guys, do you realize this is more than Nike pays any athlete in salary, even Jordan?"

Silence.

"Finally," Norton says now, recalling that morning, "Tiger says, 'Mmmm-hmmm,' and I say, 'That's it? Mmmm-hmmm?' No 'Omigod.' No slapping five or 'Ya-hooo!' So I say, 'Let me go through this again, guys.' Finally Tiger says, 'Guess that's pretty amazing.' That's it. When I made the deal with Titleist a day later, I went back to them saying, 'I'm almost embarrassed to tell you this one. Titleist is offering a little more than $20 million over five years.'"

On the Monday morning after his first pro tournament, a week after the two megadeals, Tiger scans the tiny print on the sports page under Milwaukee Open money earnings and finds his name. Tiger Woods: $2,544. "That's my money," he exclaims. "I earned this!"

See, maybe Tiger can win.

How? How can he win when there are so many insects under so many rocks? Several more death threats arrive just before the Skins Game, prompting an increase in his plain-clothes security force, which is already larger than anyone knows. His agent's first instinct is to trash every piece of hate mail delivered to IMG, but Tiger won't permit it. Every piece of racist filth must be saved and given to him. At Stanford he kept one letter taped to his wall. Fuel comes in the oddest forms.

The audience, in its hunger for goodness, swallows hard over the Nike ad that heralds Tiger's entrance into the pro-fessional ranks. The words that flash on the screen over images of Tiger—There are still courses in the United States I am not allowed to play because of the color of my skin. I've heard I'm not ready for you. Are you ready for me?—ooze the very attitude from which many in the audi-ence are seeking relief. The media backlash is swift: The Tiger Woods who used to tell the press, "The only time I think about race is when the media ask me"—whoa, what happened to him?

What happened to him was a steady accretion of experi-ences, also known as a life. What happened, just weeks before he was born, was a fusillade of limes and BBs rattling the Woods house in Cypress, Calif., one of the limes shat-tering the kitchen window, splashing glass all around the pregnant Tida, to welcome the middle-class subdivision's first non-Caucasian family.

What happened was a gang of older kids seizing Tiger on his first day of kindergarten, tying him to a tree, hurling rocks at him, calling him monkey and nigger. And Tiger, at age five, telling no one what happened for several days, trying to absorb what this meant about himself and his world.

What happened was the Look, as Tiger and Earl came to call it, the uneasy, silent stare they received in countless country-club locker rooms and restaurants. "Something a white person could never understand," says Tiger, "unless he went to Africa and suddenly found himself in the middle of a tribe." What happened was Tiger's feeling pressured to leave a driving range just two years ago, not far from his family's California home, because a resident watching Tiger's drives rocket into the nearby protective netting reported that a black teenager was trying to bombard his house.

What happened was the cold shoulder Earl got when he took his tyke to play at the Navy Golf Course in Cypress—"a club," Earl says, "composed mostly of retired naval personnel who knew blacks only as cooks and servers, and along comes me, a retired lieutenant colonel outranking 99 percent of them, and I have the nerve to take up golf at 42 and immediately become a low handicap and beat them, and then I have the audacity to have this kid. Well, they had to do something. They took away Tiger's playing privileges twice, said he was too young, even though there were other kids too young who they let play. The second time it happened, I went up to the pro who had done it and made a bet. I said, 'If you'll spot my three-year-old just one stroke a hole, nine holes, playing off the same tees, and he beats you, will you certify him?' The pro started laughing and said, 'Sure.' Tiger beat him by two strokes, got certified, then the members went over the pro's head and kicked him out again. That's when we switched him to another course."

Beat them. That was his parents' solution for each banishment, each Look. Hold your tongue, hew to every rule and beat them. Tiger Woods is the son of the first black baseball player in the Big Seven, a catcher back in the early '50s, before the conference became the Big Eight. A man who had to leave his Kansas State teammates on road trips and travel miles to stay in motels for blacks; who had to go to the back door of restaurant kitchens to be fed while his teammates dined inside; who says, "This is the most racist society in the world—I know that." A man who learned neither to extinguish his anger nor spray it but to quietly convert it into animus, the determination to enter the system and overcome it by turning its own tools against it. A Green Berets explosives expert whose mind naturally ran that way, whose response, upon hearing Tiger rave about the security in his new walled community, was, "I could get in. I could blow up the clubhouse and be gone before they ever knew what hit them." A father who saw his son, from the beginning, as the one who would enter one of America's last

Caucasian bastions, the PGA Tour, and overthrow it from within in a manner that would make it smile and ask for more. "Been planning that one for 20 years," says Earl. "See, you don't turn it into hatred. You turn it into something positive. So many athletes who reach the top now had things happen to them as children that created hostility, and they bring that hostility with them. But that hostility uses up energy. If you can do it without the chip on the shoulder, it frees up all that energy to create."

It's not until Stanford, where Tiger takes an African-American history course and stays up half the night in dormitories talking with people of every shade of skin, that his experiences begin to crystallize. "What I realized is that even though I'm mathematically Asian—if anything—if you have one drop of black blood in the United States, you're black," says Tiger. "And how important it is for this country to talk about this subject. It's not me to blow my horn, the way I come across in that Nike ad, or to say things quite that way. But I felt it was worth it because the message needed to be said. You can't say something like that in a polite way. Golf has shied away from this for too long. Some clubs have brought in tokens, but nothing has really changed. I hope what I'm doing can change that."

But don't overestimate race's proportion in the fuel that propels Tiger Woods. Don't look for traces of race in the astonishing rubble at his feet on the Sunday after he lost the Texas Open by two strokes and returned to his hotel room and snapped a putter in two with one violent lift of his knee. Then another putter. And another. And another and another—eight in all before his rage was spent and he was ready to begin considering the loss's philosophical lesson. "That volcano of competitive fire, that comes from me," says Earl. A volcano that's mostly an elite athlete's need to win, a need far more immediate than that of changing the world.

No, don't overestimate race, but don't overlook it, either. When Tiger is asked about racism, about the effect it has on him when he senses it in the air, he has a golf club in his hands. He takes the club by the neck, his eyes flashing hot and cold at once, and gives it a short upward thrust. He says, "It makes me want to stick it right up their asses." Pause. "On the golf course."

The machine will win because there is so much of the old man's breath in the boy. . . and how long can the old man keep breathing? At 2 a.m., hours before the second round of the Tour Championship in Tulsa on Oct. 25, the phone rings in Tiger's hotel room. It's Mom. Pop's in an ambulance, on his way to a Tulsa hospital. He's just had his second heart attack.

The Tour Championship? The future of humanity? The hell with 'em. Tiger's at the old man's bedside in no time, awake most of the night. Tiger's out of contention in the Tour Championship by dinnertime, with a second-round 78, his worst till then as a pro. "There are things more important than golf," he says.

The old man survives—and sees the pattern at work, of course. He's got to throw away the cigarettes. He's got to quit ordering the cholesterol special for breakfast. "I've got to shape up now, God's telling me," Earl says, "or I won't be around for the last push, the last lesson." The one about how to ride the tsunami of runaway fame.

The machine will win because no matter how complicated it all seems now, it is simpler than it will ever be. The boy will marry one day, and the happiness of two people will lie in his hands. Children will follow, and it will become his job to protect three or four or five people from the molars of the machine. Imagine the din of the grinding in five, 10, 15 years, when the boy reaches his golfing prime.

The machine will win because the whole notion is so ludicrous to begin with, a kid clutching an eight-iron changing the course of humanity. No, of course not, there won't be thousands of people sitting in front of tanks because of Tiger Woods. He won't bring about the overthrow of a tyranny or spawn a religion that one day will number 300 million devotees.

But maybe Pop is onto something without quite seeing what it is. Maybe it has to do with timing: the appearance of his son when America is turning the corner to a century in which the country's faces of color will nearly equal those that are white. Maybe, every now and then, a man gets swallowed by the machine, but the machine is changed more than he is.

For when we swallow Tiger Woods, the yellow-black-red-white man, we swallow something much more significant than Jordan or Charles Barkley. We swallow hope in the

American experiment, in the pell-mell jumbling of genes. We swallow the belief that the face of the future is not necessarily a bitter or bewildered face; that it might even, one day, be something like Tiger Woods's face: handsome and smiling and ready to kick all comers' asses.

We see a woman, 50-ish and Caucasian, well-coiffed and tailored—the woman we see at every country club—walk up to Tiger Woods before he receives the Haskins Award and say, "When I watch you taking on all those other players, Tiger, I feel like I'm watching my own son". . . and we feel the quivering of the cosmic compass that occurs when human beings look into the eyes of someone of another color and see their own flesh and blood.

Sports Illustrated, December 23, 1996

SO YOUNG TO HAVE
THE MASTER'S TOUCH

Dave Kindred

From this day forward, Tiger Woods must wear an eye patch. Before each putt, he must say "Mother, may I?" and hop three times and putt while both feet are in the air. Former girlfriends will be invited inside the gallery ropes and encouraged to recite embarrassments at the top of Tiger's backswing. He must hit every wood shot without removing that tiger head cover. He can use any ball he wants as long as it has a red stripe around it. Roseanne will be his caddie.

Stern measures, yes.

But stern measures are called for.

Or the world of golf will never be the same.

Every fifth hole, his playing partner can break the Tiger club of his choice. Tiger must play in rain falling from a movie company's giant sprinkler while everyone else plays in the sunshine. Which means Tiger will wear a raincoat and galoshes while holding an umbrella. If, despite these measures, he still gets under par, he must finish the round using a hand trowel and pool cue.

One day at a tournament in California, Tiger Woods got steamed. Somebody in the crowd had clicked off a camera just as Tiger prepared to hit a shot. "How would you like it," he snapped at the offending citizen, "if I came into your office while you're working and fired a shotgun over your head? That's what that sounds like to me out here."

Hmmm. A shotgun fired over his head. Now, there's an idea.

Just having fun here, folks. What Tiger Woods did in the Masters is so surreal as to invite hallucination.

The newest American hero has won the grand old tournament. At 21, the youngest champion ever, he won with a record score and record margin by playing golf seldom imagined let alone realized. He hit shots so far, so straight, so high and with such majesty as to leave mere mortals believing they should apologize for their miserable efforts in his supranatural company.

"Incredible," Jack Nicklaus said. . . . "A boy among men—and the boy showed the men how to play," Tom Watson said. . . . "Unbelievable," said Charlie Yates, 83, a friend of the sainted Bobby Jones who invented the Masters. And what would Bobby himself have thought? "I'm telling you," Yates said. "Unbelievable."

And the golf records themselves were the least of Tiger's accomplishment. More important than any numbers was one color. The color of his skin. The son of a Thai mother and African-American father, Tiger Woods is the first man of color to win one of golf's four major championships.

And he did it at the best place to do it if you wanted folks to sit up and take notice. He did it in a Georgia town at a tournament that for so long, either by design or circumstance, was closed to blacks. Those people who saw design at work were often moved to anger. Calvin Peete came to the Masters in 1980, the second black player in the tournament's history, and he once said, "Asking me if I enjoy being here is like asking if we enjoyed slavery."

A different time now. Different perspectives. For Peete and for the first black player, Lee Elder, the Masters came with a plantation feel. For good reason considering the place and the time—the American South in the 20th century—the Elders and Peetes thought of themselves as field hands who were allowed, briefly, to visit the massah's big house.

But now comes Tiger Woods with the shoe company's $40 million deal, Tiger Woods who has never been a field hand, Tiger Woods who has led a privileged life. Calvin Peete sold jewelry out of his car trunk to migrant workers in Florida until, past 30, he made a dime playing golf. Lee Elder rode country highways with the famous hustler

Titanic Thompson, the old man and the black kid teeing it up against anyone foolish enough to mistake age and color for weakness.

And now comes Tiger Woods. His swing is silken beauty rather than a clanking assemblage of spare parts put together on hardpan goat hills. And he speaks not of anger but of what a victory can do for people, young minorities especially, who might be moved by his victory to try the game.

Lee Elder first came to Augusta in 1975. He was 40. He came again at 62 for Tiger Woods. He came on Sunday morning when the kid would win. Under the mighty oak trees by Augusta National's clubhouse, Elder said, "Tiger Woods wins here, it might have more significance than Jackie Robinson's break into baseball. No one will turn their head when a black man walks to the first tee."

Then Elder moved to a practice area to speak to Woods, a moment Woods liked. "He was the first," Woods said. "He was the one I looked up to." Then he called a roll of men excluded by the fact of their color, Elder and Charlie Sifford and Ted Rhodes. "Because of them, I was able to play on the PGA Tour. I was able to live my dream because of those guys."

Now comes Tiger Woods, the one and only.

And we'll see what it means. "A lot of kids will start playing," he said, "and over time, hopefully, I'll be around to see the fruits of the things I've accomplished. . . . I think that now kids will think golf is cool, really."

And make no mistake about Tiger Woods, the competitor. He knows history and he chases it. His is a dream dreamed large. For the first time ever, so powerful was Woods' work, it is reasonable to think of a man winning all four majors in a year, the Grand Slam. The question was put to Woods this way: "Tiger, how soon is a slam?"

The clever champ smiled. "A slam dunk?"

Then he said the right things about how difficult such a feat would be, how much luck would be required, how many great players there are. All of which he wrapped around one meaningful sentence.

"I think it can be done," he said.

Yes, the world of golf is about to be born anew.

Sporting News, April 21, 1997

TIGER WOODS
GOES FOR THE GREEN

Maureen Dowd

There have been other disses of historic proportion.

There was the time the wife of Mayor Ralph Perk of Cleveland turned down an invitation to a Nixon White House dinner because it was her bowling night.

Still, as snubs go, this one was pretty impressive.

The leader of the free world offered to send an Air Force plane to pick up Tiger Woods so he could come to Shea Stadium to honor Jackie Robinson, the most important African-American athlete in history.

It would have been an amazing moment: the new legend who effortlessly broke a color line in golf taking a moment to genuflect to the old legend who courageously broke the color line in baseball 50 years earlier.

But the 21-year-old who is often described as the Jackie Robinson of golf blew off Jackie Robinson—and the Fan in Chief. He had more pressing matters, following his dazzling Masters triumph.

On Monday he flew to Myrtle Beach, S.C., and Atlantic City to snip ribbons at the openings of Official All-Star Cafes, which he owns with other sports stars. He also had to powwow with his agent, Hughes Norton of IMG Sports Marketing, about a cascade of sponsorship offers that could go nicely with his $60 million Nike and Titleist deals and his plans for Tiger Woods watches, sportswear, golf clubs and autobiography. On Tuesday he took off for a vacation in Mexico with a couple of old Stanford buddies.

"There's no bigger hero to anybody than Jackie Robinson is to Tiger Woods," says Norton. "But the president's request would have required Tiger being in Mexico on Wednesday noon instead of Tuesday morning."

John Feinstein, who wrote *A Good Walk Spoiled: Days and Nights on the PGA Tour* and who refers to IMG as "I Am Greedy," thought Woods' decision not to go sullied the elegance of his Masters tribute to older black players. "I guess he feels, with some justification, that right now he's bulletproof," he said.

GQ magazine wrote that the selling of Tiger Woods by IMG and his father has been offensively messianic. At first, Tiger emphasized his multiracial background. But then his management team and Nike decided to push him as a healer who could change the world, "a racial pioneer along the lines of Jackie Robinson, Muhammad Ali and Arthur Ashe."

It is perplexing why a young man with such a long "shelf life," as his agent puts it, could not have paused on the merchandising mania for a couple of days. After all, he says he is eager to be a role model. But on second thought, by putting himself ahead of history, he is a role model for what our society cares about.

President Clinton brought this on himself. He has done the political equivalent of an athlete plastering himself with sponsorship logos. He has tirelessly marketed the presidency and piggybacked on the aura of Olympians and celebrity athletes.

Woods probably sees the president as just one more person trying to cash in. Norton said that when Clinton was on his Australian tour last December, Woods got several calls from the White House asking if he would consider playing a round of golf with the president. But before final arrangements were made, Clinton showed up on the links with Greg Norman.

"Tiger found it a little curious that he wasn't important enough to be with the president until he won the Masters," Norton said.

With one swat at a president who is a lame duck, a grand jury magnet and a groupie, Woods made it clear who is the more valuable commodity.

"We talked about the pros and cons. Hey, this will be perceived as snubbing the president . . ." Norton said. "But this is really a tribute to Tiger Woods's single-mindedness and individuality that he was able to say, 'Hey, this is something that's been scheduled for a long time.'"

These two guys should get together on the green. They have a lot in common. And it's green.

New York Times, April 22, 1997

THE MAN, AMEN

Charles P. Pierce

OK. Golf joke.

Jesus Christ and Saint Peter go out to play golf. Saint Peter steps up to the first tee. He's got the sharp designer vines. Even got a brand-new yellow Amana hat. (Amana sewed up a sponsorship deal long before anyone else, and Nike couldn't even get in the door.) Clubheads that gleam in the heavenly light like stars on sticks. Takes out a golden tee. Puts down a fresh Titleist Balata. Smacks it down the fairway for a clean 265, dead center. Ball sits in the green grass like a distant white diamond. Allows himself a little smirk as he steps out of the tee box. Listens carefully to hear if a cock is crowing.

Anyway, Jesus up next. Old robe. Sawdust up to his elbows (somebody needed a coffee table finished that morning). Got a black rock tied to a cane pole. Got a range ball with a red stripe around its middle and a deep slice up one side. Hits the ball with the rock, and it goes straight up in the air. It is plucked away by a passing pileated wood-pecker, which flaps off down the fairway toward the green. Stiff head wind blows up. Woodpecker begins to labor. Just over the front fringe of the green, woodpecker suffers a fatal heart attack. Drops the ball onto the back of a passing box turtle. Ball sticks. Turtle carries the ball toward the hole. At the lip of the cup, turtle sneezes.

Ball drops into the hole.

Saint Peter shakes his head.

"You gonna play golf?" he asks Jesus. "Or you gonna fuck around?"

Is this blasphemous?

Is it?

Truly blasphemous?

Truly?

And what would be the blasphemy?

And what would it be?

The punch line? That Saint Peter is said to be using a curse word as regards his Lord and Savior?

No, ma'am. Sorry. Please consult Matthew 26:73–74.

And after a little while, they came that stood by, and they said to Peter, "Surely, thou art one of them, for even thy speech doth discover thee."

Then he began to curse and to swear that he knew not the man.

And immediately the cock crowed.

Peter was forgiven.
And what would be the blasphemy?
And what would it be?
That our Lord and Savior would play golf?
That He would do anything within His admittedly considerable powers to win?
No, ma'am. Sorry. I believe that Jesus would play to win. I would not want Jesus in a $1,000 Nassau, not even with four shots a side. I do not like my chances at that. No, ma'am, I do not. I believe Jesus would take my money. I believe that He would take it and give it unto the poor, but I believe He would take it. I believe that Jesus would focus. I believe that His ball would not find the rough. I believe that there would be sudden windstorms. I believe that He would find no water, but that if He did, He would walk out and knock one stiff from the middle of the pond. I believe that He would go for the stick on every hole. I believe that the Redeemer cometh and He playeth to win, or else He'd have wound up as merely one of the foremost carpenters in Nazareth. I would not want Jesus in a $1,000 Nassau, not even with four shots a side.
Is this blasphemous?
Is it?
And what would be the blasphemy?
And what would it be?
That there is divinity guiding the game of golf? That the hands of God are on a steel shaft, the fingers of God over-

lapped and strong, and that the hands of God bring the steel shaft up brightly in the heavenly light—but not past parallel; never past parallel—and then down, hard, to smite the sinful modern world?

Is this blasphemous?

Is it?

In the limo, fresh from a terribly wearisome photo shoot that may only help get him laid about 296 times in the next calendar year, if he so chooses, the Redeemer is pondering one of the many mysteries of professional sports.

"What I can't figure out," Tiger Woods asks Vincent, the limo driver, "is why so many good-looking women hang around baseball and basketball. Is it because, you know, people always say that, like, black guys have big dicks?"

Vincent says nothing right off. Vincent is cool. Vincent played college ball at Memphis State under Dana Kirk, and that is like saying that you rode the range with Jesse James or prowled the White House with Gordon Liddy. Straight outlaw street creds, no chaser. Vincent is sharp. Vincent got into computers back when computers meant Univac, and that is like saying you got into navigation when navigation meant Columbus. Vincent is cool and Vincent is sharp, but Vincent is stumped here for an answer.

He and Tiger have already discussed video games. Tiger likes fighting games. He has no patience for virtual skate-boarding. "I get fucking pissed when I've got a station and no games to play on it. It's frustrating," Tiger said. He and Tiger have also discussed the various models of Mercedes automobiles. The day before, Tiger won himself a new Mercedes automobile at a golf tournament outside San Diego. But it was such an ordinary, respectable Mercedes that Tiger gave it to his mother. Tiger likes the more formidable model of Mercedes that Ken Griffey Jr. drives. "That is a great fucking car, man," he enthused. Vincent agreed. But then Tiger came up with this question about why all the good-looking women follow baseball and basketball, and he came up with this theory about black men and their big dicks, and Vincent is not ready for the turn that the conversation has taken.

So I step in. It is said to be the case, I begin, trying to give Vincent a moment to regroup, that women follow baseball and basketball closely because those two sports put them in greater proximity to the players.

"What about golf then?" says Tiger, and now I am stumped for an answer.

Vincent finally tells him, "Well, what Mr. Pierce back there says is right, and what you said, well, there's probably some truth to that, too. And the other thing is that there is so much money involved in those two sports that that probably has something to do with it, too." Tiger seems very satisfied with the roundness of this answer. He says nothing for a moment. He looks out the window of the limousine, and he watches the failed condominium developments go passing by.

One day earlier, he had won the Mercedes Championships at the La Costa Resort and Spa. La Costa was the place into which the Mob plowed all that money from the

Teamsters pension fund. La Costa is now owned by the Japanese. Jimmy Hoffa must be spinning in the Meadowlands. The Mercedes Championships used to be what the PGA Tour called the Tournament of Champions. All things do change. Still, only golfers who have won a tour event during the previous season are eligible to play in this tournament, which annually kicks off the new tour season. In 1996 Tiger qualified for the Mercedes by winning two of the eight tournaments he entered after joining the tour in September.

At La Costa on Saturday, he birdied the last four holes to move into a tie with Tom Lehman, the 1996 PGA Tour player of the year. On Sunday, however, La Costa was drenched by a winter storm out of the Pacific, and it was determined that Lehman and Woods would play a one-hole play-off for the championship, the $296,000 first prize and the brand-new Mercedes. The official chose the par-three seventh hole, which ran off an elevated tee down to a green bounded by water on the left side. Hundreds of people scurried down through the rain, a great army moving behind a screen of trees, a bustling little loop of humanity shivering under bright umbrellas.

Lehman hit first. He caught his shot fat. It landed on the far bank and hopped backward into the pond, scattering a flock of American coots. (These were genuine American coots—also called mud hens—and not the other, more visibly affluent American coots, some of whom were lining the fairway.) Now, there was virtually no way for Woods to lose the tournament. He could reverse pivot and line up the clubhouse veranda, and he'd still be better off than poor Lehman, who had to function amid the ragged and distant hosannas of Tiger's partisans cheering Lehman's misfortune. Instead, Woods took out a seven-iron. As he followed through, a raindrop fell in his eye, partly blinding him.

The ball damned near went in the hole.

The crowd—his crowd, always his crowd now—did not cheer. Not at first. Instead, what the crowd did was . . . sag. There was a brief, precious slice of time in which the disbelief was sharp and palpable, even in the pulping winter rain. Then the cheers came, and they did not stop until he'd reached the green. He tapped in for the championship, the check and the car, which he gave to his mother.

"All right, here's what happened," Tiger would explain later. "If I hit it toward the middle of the green and my natural draw takes over, then I should be right at the hole. If I hit the iron shot I'd been hitting all week, which was kind of a weak-ass shot to the right, then it should hold against the wind and make it dead straight.

"So I turned it over perfect. I finally hit my natural shot."

And how long did all this calculating take?

"A couple of seconds. Of course, if he'd have hit it close, I probably would've been more aggressive."

The next morning—this morning—a limousine picked him up at his mother's house, and it took him to a photo shoot for the magazine cover that is only going to get him laid 296 times in the next year, if he so chooses. He gave the photographer an hour. One single hour. Sixty minutes, flat, in front of the camera. In the studio, which was wedged into a Long Beach alley behind a copy store and next to Andre's Detailing Shop (if you happen to need an Aztec firebird on your hood in a hurry, Andre's your man), Tiger was dressed in very sharp clothes by four lovely women who attended to his every need and who flirted with him at about warp nine. Tiger responded. Tiger told us all some jokes.

This is one of the jokes that Tiger told:

The Little Rascals are at school. The teacher wants them to use various words in sentences. The first word is *love*. Spanky answers, "I love dogs." The second word is *respect*. Alfalfa answers, "I respect how much Spanky loves dogs." The third word is *dictate*. There is a pause in the room. Finally, Buckwheat puts up his hand.

"Hey, Darla," says Buckwheat. "How my dick ta'te?"

He was rolling now. The women were laughing. They were also still flirting. The clothes were sharp, and the photographer was firing away like the last machine gunner at Passchendaele. And Tiger told jokes. Tiger has not been 21 years old for a month yet, and he tells jokes that most 21-year-olds would tell around the keg in the dormitory late on a Saturday night. He tells jokes that a lot of arrested 45-year-olds will tell at the clubhouse bar as the gin begins to soften Saturday afternoon into Saturday evening.

This is one of the jokes that Tiger told:

He puts the tips of his expensive shoes together, and he rubs them up and down against each other. "What's this?" he asks the women, who do not know the answer.

"It's a black guy taking off his condom," Tiger explains.

He tells jokes that are going to become something else entirely when they appear in this magazine because he is not most 21-year-olds, and because he is not going to be a 45-year-old club pro with a nose spidered red and hands palsied with the gin yips in the morning, and because—through his own efforts, the efforts of his father, his management team and his shoe company, and through some of the most bizarre sporting prose ever concocted—he's become the center of a secular cult, the tenets of which hold that something beyond golf is at work here, something that will help redeem golf from its racist past, something that will help redeem America from its racist past, something that will bring a new era of grace and civility upon the land, and something that will, along the way, produce in Tiger Woods the greatest golfer in the history of the planet. It has been stated—flatly, and by people who ought to know better—that the hand of God is working through Tiger Woods in order to make this world a better place for us all.

Is that blasphemous?

Is it?

There is no place in the gospel of the church of Tiger Woods for jokes like this one:

Why do two lesbians always get where they're going faster than two gay guys?

Because the lesbians are always going sixty-nine.

Is that blasphemous?

Is it?

It is an interesting question, one that was made sharper when Tiger looked at me and said, "Hey, you can't write this."

"Too late," I told him, and I was dead serious, but everybody laughed because everybody knows there's no place in the gospel of Tiger for these sorts of jokes. And Tiger gave the photographer his hour, and we were back in the car with Vincent and heading back toward Tiger's mother's house. "Well, what did you think of the shoot?" Tiger asks, yawning, because being ferried by a limousine and being handled by beautiful women and being photographed for a magazine cover that will get him laid 296 times in the next year, if he so chooses, can be very exhausting work. "The key to it," he says, "is to give them a time and to stick to it. If I say I'm there for an hour, I'm there, on time, for an hour. If they ask for more, I say, 'Hell, fuck no.' And I'm out of there."

Hell, fuck no?

Is that blasphemous?

Is it?

And what would the blasphemy be?

And what would it be?

Can he blaspheme against his own public creation, his own unique role, as determined by his father, his management team and his shoe company? Can he blaspheme

against the image coddled and nurtured by the paid evan-
gelists of his own gospel?

Hell, fuck no?

And what would the blasphemy be?

And what would it be?

Can he blaspheme against himself?

God willing, he can.

Two days earlier, while Tiger's father was greeting passersby
behind the ninth green at La Costa, Tida Woods was following Tiger around the course. She is a small, bustling
woman who occasionally is forced to take a little hop in
order to see over the spectators in front of her. On the fif-
teenth hole, Tiger left his approach shot short of the green.

"Well," Tida said, "Tiger will chip this one in, and we'll
go to the next hole."

Tiger chipped the ball, which bounced twice and rolled
straight into the cup.

"That boy," said Tida Woods. "I told you he would do
that."

She walked on. I stood stunned under a tree for a very
long time and wondered about what I had just seen. I think
there are pilgrims at Lourdes who look like I did.

This is what I believe about Tiger Woods. These are the
articles of my faith.

I believe that he is the best golfer under the age of 30
that there ever has been. I believe that he is going to be the

best golfer of any age that there ever has been. I believe that he is going to win more tournaments than Jack Nicklaus won. I believe that he is going to win more major championships than Jack Nicklaus won, and I believe that both of these records are going to stand for Tiger Woods longer than they have stood for Jack Nicklaus. I believe he is going to be rich and famous, and I believe that he is going to bring great joy to a huge number of people because of his enormous talent on the golf course. This is what I believe about Tiger Woods. These are the articles of my faith.

I believe that he is the most charismatic athlete alive today. I believe that his charisma comes as much from the way he plays the game as it does from the way he looks and from what he is supposed to symbolize. I believe that his golf swing—never past parallel—is the most perfect golf swing yet devised. I believe that he is longer off the tee than any good player ever has been, and I believe he is a better player than anyone else longer off the tee. This is what I believe about Tiger Woods. These are the articles of my faith.

I believe that Tiger Woods is as complete a cutthroat as has ever played golf. I do not want Tiger Woods in a $1,000 Nassau, not even with forty shots a side. I believe he would take my money. I believe I would leave the course wearing a barrel. I believe that the shot that won for him at La Costa was not completely about beating Tom Lehman on that afternoon, because Tiger could have used a lemon zester to do that. I believe that shot was for a couple of weeks or a year from now, when Lehman is trying to hold a one-shot lead over Tiger Woods down the stretch in a major tournament. This is what I believe about Tiger Woods. These are the articles of my faith.

This is what I do not believe about Tiger Woods. These are the theses of my heresy.

I do not believe that Tiger Woods was sent to us for any mission other than that of "being a great golfer and a better person," as his father puts it. After all, this is the mission we all have, except for the golf part. (No just and merciful God would demand as the price of salvation that we all learn to hit a one-iron.) I do not believe that a higher power is working through Tiger Woods and the International Management Group, even though IMG once represented the incumbent pope. I do not believe that a higher power is working through Tiger Woods and the Nike corporation:

Tiger, Tiger, burning bright
Selling shoes for Philip Knight

This is what I do not believe about Tiger Woods. These are the theses of my heresy. I do not believe the following sentence, which appears in one of several unauthorized hagiographies: "I don't think he is a god, but I do believe that he was sent by one." This sentence presumes, first, that there is a God and, second, that He busies himself in the manufacture of professional golfers for the purpose of redeeming the various sinful regions of the world. I do not believe this about Tiger Woods.

I do not believe what was said about Tiger by his father in the issue of *Sports Illustrated* in which Tiger Woods was named the Sportsman of the Year: "*Can't you see the pattern? Earl Woods asks. Can't you see the signs?* 'Tiger will do more than any other man in history to change the course of humanity,' Earl says."

I do not believe that Earl Woods knows God's mind. I do not believe that Earl Woods could find God's mind with a pack of bloodhounds and Thomas Aquinas leading the way. I do not believe that God's mind can be found on a golf course as though it were a flock of genuine American coots. I do not believe—right now, this day—that Tiger Woods will change humanity any more than Chuck Berry did. This is what I do not believe about Tiger Woods. These are the theses of my heresy.

Is that blasphemy?

Is it?

In the beginning was the father.

"I said," Earl Woods insisted, "that Tiger had the ability to be one of the biggest influences in history. I didn't say that he would be. I am not in the business of predicting the next Messiah, nor do I feel that Tiger *is* the next Messiah. That's stupid. That's just stupid."

Earl Woods was a tired man. He had walked the back fairways of La Costa, where he was treated by his son's galleries the way that mobsters used to be greeted by the doormen at this place. But he'd forgotten his folding chair, and he'd forgotten his CD player on which he listens to his jazz music while Tiger plays. He was a month away from bypass surgery, and he was beginning to get cranky about it.

"I'm a terrible patient," he said. "I'm one of those people who say, 'I don't want to be here.' And then I make such an ass of myself that people let me go. They don't have any reason to keep me."

The story of Earl and his son is worn nearly smooth by now. How Earl fought in Indochina as a Green Beret alongside a South Vietnamese named Nguyen Phong, whom everyone called Tiger. How Earl returned from the war with a Thai wife named Kultida, and how they had a child whom Tida named Eldrick—"Fathers are just along for the ride on that one," Earl explained—but upon whom Earl insisted on bestowing his old comrade's nickname. How Earl would take the toddler with him when he went to hit golf balls. How the little boy climbed out of the high chair and swiped at the ball himself, showing superlative form. And how everything came from that—the appearance on television with Mike Douglas when Tiger was only 3, the superlative junior amateur career, the three consecutive U.S. Amateur titles, the explosion onto the PGA Tour at the end of last season.

And it was Earl's apparently limitless capacity for metaphysical hooey and sociological bunkum that produced the gospel that has so entranced the world, the golfing press and large conglomerate industries. Separated into its component parts, Earl's gospel is predestination theory heavily marbled with a kind of Darwinist Christianity and leavened with Eastern mysticism. Simply put, the gospel has it that while Earl Woods was wandering through Indochina, a divine plan was put in motion by which Earl would one day have a son who would win a lot of golf tournaments and make a lot of money because it was his karma to do so, and that, through doing this, the son would change the world itself.

"I think that the SI article went a little too deep," Tiger muses. "As writers go, you guys try to dig deep into something that is really nothing." Well, perhaps, but Earl certainly said what he said, and Tiger certainly has profited, because the promulgation of Earl's gospel is as much at the heart of Tiger's appeal as is his ability to go long off the tee.

There is a dodgy sense of transition around Tiger now, a feeling that the great plates on which he has built his career have begun to shift. In December, for example, he and his father fired John Merchant, Tiger's longtime attorney. Moreover, there is a sense among the other people on Tiger's management team that Earl has pushed his own celebrity far beyond the limits of discretion, particularly in his comments to SI concerning Tiger's place in the world. At La Costa, after Tiger's round on Saturday, his swing coach, Butch Harmon, dropped by the press room to cadge a beer.

"Earl," he said with a huge sigh, "is getting out of control."

This is not something anyone would have dared to say even a year ago.

It is perhaps understandable. By his play and by the shrewd marketing that has surrounded his career almost from the time he could walk, Tiger Woods is now an authentic phenomenon. Golf tournaments in which he plays sell more than twice the number of tickets they would if he did not. With Michael Jordan heading toward eclipse and with no other successor on the horizon, Tiger Woods is going to be the most popular athlete in the world for a very long time. The old support system worked splendidly as he came up through the amateur ranks. But there are unmistakable signs that it has become seriously overtaxed.

Consider, for example, the persistent rumors that Earl and Tida have all but separated. At La Costa, they were not seen together on the course at all. Tida commuted to her new house, while Earl stayed at the resort. (At the time, IMG insisted that any rumors of a split were not true.) There was no evidence in his room that she had been there at all. There was only Earl, alone in the room, suffused with a kind of blue melancholy, an old man now, and tired besides.

"I'll be satisfied if he's just a great person," Earl says. "I don't give a shit about the golf."

Ah, but he does. He has given up a lot for it. He left another wife and three other children. He has devoted his life, a lot of his energy and a great deal of surpassing bullshit to creating something that may now be moving far out of his control. "I'm not worried now," he says. "Obviously, I will not be here to see the final result. I will see enough to know that I've done a good job."

On the first day at La Costa, Tiger was paired with David Ogrin, a veteran tour pro who'd won the previous year's Texas Open, his first victory after fourteen years and 405 tournaments. Ogrin is considered one of the tour's most enlightened citizens despite the fact that he looks like a rodeo bouncer and is the owner of one of America's most genuinely red necks. The two of them reached the ninth tee. Tiger had the honors. He absolutely scalded the ball down the center of the fairway, yards beyond anyone else who would play the hole that day.

"Hey," said David Ogrin in awe and wonder. "Eat me."

It was Butch Harmon's time of day. The son of a Masters champion and the brother of three other PGA pros, Harmon was stalking the practice tee at La Costa in the mist of the early morning. He explained how much of Tiger's power comes from his longer musculature—"almost like a track athlete," he said. "Tiger was born with a beautiful natural flow to his swing. It enables him to come through the ball almost like the crack of a whip. Add to that the fact that he was taught well early, because Earl had a real good concept of the golf swing." And then he said something else—something beyond mechanics, but just as important.

"You know, you can get so wrapped up in this game that you have no fun, and as soon as you know it, your career is over and you never had any," he said. "It's a game you can get so serious on that you can't . . . *play.*"

It is the golf that is the sweetest thing about Tiger's story. It is the golf that is free of cant and manufactured import. To the untutored, Tiger Woods is an appealing golfer because he is young and fresh, and because of the distances he can carry with a golf ball. To the purist, he is appealing because his swing is the purest distillation of Everyman's swing. Unlike John Daly, who approaches a golf ball with a club in much the way Mel Gibson approached English infantrymen with a broadsword, Tiger has a swing that is both controlled and clean. "I never go past parallel," he says. "I think people look at me and say, 'That's the way I want to hit the ball.'"

There was resistance to him on the tour at first, because he had come so far so young. But what overcame that was Tiger's manifest hunger to compete. It is not artificial. It is not feigned. It is real and genuine and very formidable. There is a difference between getting up in the morning to win and getting up to *beat* people. Tiger's gospel says that he has more of the first kind of days than he has of the second. The reality is far less clear. He didn't have to go after the pin on Lehman. But he did. "It's nice to know you're out there with somebody whose sole goal isn't to make third on the money list," says Justin Leonard, a gifted young pro.

"I just love to compete," Tiger says. "I don't care if it's golf or Nintendo or in the classroom. I mean, competing against the other students or competing against myself. I know what I'm capable of.

"You know, the prize money, that's the paycheck. That's the money I earned for myself. All the other stuff, my Nike contract and Titleist and now the All Star Cafe, to me, that's a bank account, but it doesn't really make me as happy as what I earn through blood, sweat and tears on the golf course. That money, I have the sole responsibility for earning that. Just me, alone. All the other stuff can depend on how good your agent is."

It's the gospel that has complicated his life. He can commit minor faux pas that become major ones because they run counter to the prefabricated Tiger of the gospel. Soon after he announced he would leave college to turn pro, Nike featured him in a commercial in which he said, "There are still courses in the United States that I am not allowed to play because of the color of my skin," and the world exploded.

The racial aspect of Tiger's gospel has always been the most complex part of it. At first he emphasized his multiracial background—after all, he is as much Thai as he is American, and Earl is an authentic American ethnic stew. At the same time, Tiger and his management team were pushing him as a racial pioneer along the lines of Jackie Robinson, Muhammad Ali and Arthur Ashe, none of whom considered themselves "multi-ethnic." The Nike commercial pointed up the dissonance of the two messages. One prominent gasbag of a pundit challenged Nike to find a course that Tiger couldn't play.

It was an interesting case study in the practical application of the gospel. In the first place, if you dressed Tiger up in ordinary golf clothes—an outfit, say, without thirty-three Nike swooshes on it—I'm willing to bet you *could* find a course in this great land of ours that wouldn't let a black man play. However, the gospel insists that Tiger came to heal and not to wound. There is no place in journalism whiter than sports writing, and there is no sports writing whiter than golf writing, and generally it is the received wisdom that to be great any great black athlete must be a figure of conciliation and not division. Witness, for example, the revolting use of Muhammad Ali in this regard, especially now that he can't speak for himself. The imperatives of the gospel held. The spot was pulled.

There is little question that Tiger has brought black fans into the game, and that he is part of a modern continuum that reaches back to Jack Johnson. Johnson was a hero generally among black people not far removed from *Plessy v. Ferguson*. Later, Joe Louis served much the same function, except that Louis was far less threatening to white people and thus had an easier time of it. (It was with Louis that we first saw white people using a black champion to prove to themselves how broad-minded they'd become.) Jackie Robinson was a hero to those black people who came north in the great migration to work in the factories in places like Brooklyn. Arthur Ashe came along at a time when the civil rights movement had begun to create a substantial black middle class. And now that America has begun to wish for the appearance of the great racial conciliator, along comes Tiger Woods.

"The reason is the timing of it," he says. "Other guys, like Charlie Sifford, they didn't get the publicity, because the era was wrong. They came along when prejudice reigned supreme. I came along at the right time."

I believe that Tiger will break the gospel before the gospel breaks him. It constricts and binds his entire life. It leaves him no room for ambiguity, no refuge in simple humanity. Earl and Tida can't break up, because the gospel has made their family into a model for the "unfortunate" broken homes that produce so many other athletes. Tiger can't fire his lawyer, because the gospel portrays him as a decent and caring young man. Tiger can't be an angry black man—not even for show, not even for money—because the gospel paints him as a gifted black man rewarded by a caring white society. Tiger can't even tell dirty jokes, because the gospel has no place for them, and they will become events if someone reports them, because, in telling them, he does it:

He blasphemes against himself.

I believe in what I saw at La Costa, a preternaturally mature young man coming into the full bloom of a staggering talent and enjoying very much nearly every damn minute of it. I watched the young women swoon behind the ropes, and I believe that Tiger noticed them, too. There was one woman dressed in a frilly lace top and wearing a pair of tiger-striped stretch pants that fit as though they were decals. I believe that Tiger noticed this preposterous woman, and I do not believe that she was Mary Magdalene come back to life.

"See her?" said one jaded tour observer. "Last year she was following Greg Norman, and there were sharks on her pants."

It is not the world of the gospel, but it is a world I can believe.

Hello, world.

The seventeenth hole at La Costa is a 569-yard par-five that the locals call the Monster. Legend had it that no professional had ever reached it in two. Back up in the tee box, Tiger was getting ready to drive the hole. He had birdied the previous two holes, hurling himself at Tom Lehman, who was still leading the tournament by two strokes. As I walked from tee toward green, I noticed a young couple standing alone, far ahead of the mass of the gallery. They had established a distinct position under a gnarled old jutting tree. The tee box was invisible back behind the crook in the dogleg. A few yards in front of the couple, a browned footpath bisected the fairway.

"This," the man explained, "is where John Daly hit it last year."

The roar came up the fairway in a ragged ripple. And I saw the heads swivel all the way back along the fairway, swivel back and then up, back and then up. And then forward, still up. Forward, still up. I found myself caught up in it, and I saw the ball passing overhead, passing the point where the couple had decided to stand, passing the point where John Daly had once hit a golf shot that no longer mattered.

The ball dropped on the other side of the little brown path. The crowd did not cheer, not instantly. The crowd simply . . . sagged. Then they cheered, and the crowd came tumbling after Tiger along the sides of the fairway. He had hit the ball past everyone's expectations.

Tiger had a birdie in his pocket, unless he jerked it over the flock of genuine American coots and dunked it into the designer pond in front of the green. All he had to do was lay it up, pitch the ball close and sink his short putt. That was the safe play. That was what he should have done.

Tiger took a wood out of his bag.

The gallery erupted.

It has been a long time since any golf gallery cheered someone for removing a club from his bag. The ovation was not about redemption or about inspiration. It was not about the metaphysical maundering of theological dilettantes. It was about courage and risk and athletic daring. Its ultimate source was irrelevant, but I do not believe this golden moment was foreordained by God while Earl Woods was stumbling around Indochina trying not to get his ass shot off. To believe that would be to diminish God.

And that would be the blasphemy.

And that's what it would be.

He needs so little of what is being put upon him. I believe in the 21-year-old who tells dirty jokes and who plays Nintendo games, and only the fighting games at that. I do not believe in the chosen one, the redeemer of golf and of America and of the rest of the world. I hope he plays golf. I hope he fucks around.

I believe he can blaspheme himself. And I hope to God he does.

These are the theses of my heresy.

"Hey, Darla. How my dick ta'te?"

And I hope the jokes will get better.

It was a savage and wonderful choice that he made, the choice of a man who competes and who knows the difference between those days when you want to win and those days when you want to beat people, and who glories in both kinds of days. The choice he made to hit the wood was a choice he made not only for that day but also for a hundred others, when other golfers will be playing him close, and they will remember what he did, and maybe, just maybe, they will jerk it over the coots and into the pond. If that is the hand of God, it is closed then into a fist.

"Because the lesbians always go sixty-nine."

They will get much better.

He took back the club—never past parallel—and it whistled down, and I could hear Butch Harmon talking softly about the crack of the whip. I heard no sound at contact. The ball rose, gleaming, into the soft blue sky. Tiger followed the flight of the ball, stone silent but smiling just a bit. The gallery began to stir as the shot easily cleared the pond and rolled up onto the green no one had ever hit in two before. The smile never made it all the way to his eyes.

This is what I believe in, finally. This is the article of my faith. I believe in that one, risky shot, and I believe in the ball, a distant white diamond in the clear heavens, and the voices that rose toward it, washed in its wake, but rising, rising still, far above the profane earth.

I believe in the prayers of the assembled congregation assembled.

"Youthemanyouthemanyouthemanyoutheman.

"God! You the fucking MAN!"

Amen.

THE LOST GENERATION

Frank Deford

You're The Second-Best Golfer in the world. You're Faldo or Price or Els or Montgomerie or Lehman or Norman or . . .

Whoever.

Whatshisname.

You're The Second-Best Golfer in the world and you thought you had a really rich contract with Titleist or Callaway or somebody, but now it's chump change compared to what HE's got.

But then, you're The Second-Best Golfer in the world and nobody even cares anymore what ball you're playing.

Or what you're wearing.

Or what you're hitting with.

Or, for that matter: what your name is.

You're The Second-Best Golfer in the world, and when the guy next to you on the airplane finds out what you do for a living, he asks you if you know HIM.

And what's HE really like?

And what's Fluff, HIS caddie, really like?

You're The Second-Best Golfer in the world and when you arrive at the tournament, everybody tells you, isn't it wonderful because HE will actually play here this week.

You're The Second-Best Golfer in the world, and while you're certainly not as stupid as Fuzzy, you are human, you're one of the boys, and did-you-hear-the-one-about, and now, can you believe this, all of a sudden, because of HIM, *you're the minority?*

You're The Second-Best Golfer in the world, and you remember when you made your first 36-hole cut at a tournament, won $640 for finishing tied for 24th place, went out and applied for an American Express card.

Now you've moved up to the Platinum card, but all of a sudden HE *is* the American Express card. And you can't even leave home without HIM.

You're The Second-Best Golfer in the world, and you hit it right on the button, perfect, right down the middle, 270 yards, and that leaves you only 60 yards short of HIM, because he kinda misplayed his drive.

But, anyway, you absolutely are The Second-Best Golfer in the world, and, after all, you're playing a game for mature, thinking men, where physical prowess is only part of the act, and you've miscalculated with the four-iron and put the approach short in the trap, whereas HE faded the eight-iron hole high, two feet straight in for the birdie.

You're The Second-Best Golfer in the world, and HE doesn't even know you're the guy paired with him today, but already you're thinking that maybe, just maybe, HE can't play a Scottish links course all that well the first time, in a few weeks, so there's at least one tournament all year I got an outside chance in.

If the wind really blows like a madman off the Firth of Forth.

And HE doesn't like the food.

You're The Second-Best Golfer in the world, and your agent keeps telling you that if you just put a little snap in your best Arnold Palmer anecdotes, you can maybe get a shot on Leno or Letterman, or, for sure, a pop on Tom Snyder . . . but HE's already done Oprah and Barbara Walters and turned down the president.

You're The Second-Best Golfer in the world, but away from a tournament city, you can't even get a good table at a steakhouse, because nobody knows you from the Culligan Man, but already HIS mother has a Q-rating higher than Tea Leoni or Craig T. Nelson and HIS father just sold his book to Miramax.

Starring Bill Cosby, no doubt. With Wilford Brimley as Fluff.

You're The Second-Best Golfer in the world and you finally got a deal to represent a resort in Florida with a certified PGA course and a mall. Already, though, HE's got a deal representing a whole country.

Thailand.

I forget: Is Asia just a tour or is it a whole continent, too?

You're The Second-Best Golfer in the world, so why are you already looking ahead to the senior tour on ESPN2?

You're The Second-Best Golfer in the world, and you've reached a point where maybe you win a couple more majors, and they mention you in the same breath as Snead or Nelson, but all of a sudden you realize nobody even heard of Snead or Nelson anymore.

Also, for that matter, now, nobody anymore ever heard of Jones or Hogan or Nicklaus.

You're The Second-Best Golfer in the world and nobody even stays still and quiet when you putt out, because they've got to run to get a good spot so they can shout "You The Man" louder than the other butt-kissing, putter-sniffing guys when HE tees off.

You're The Second-Best Golfer in the world, longtime par-busting star of the tour, and suddenly you realize there is no "tour." It is just HIS show.

But then, you're The Second-Best Golfer in the world, and suddenly you understand: there is no second-best golfer in the world.

And, you're the second-best golfer in all the world of golf, and then you realize there is no golf anymore. It is just HIM, playing around.

It is just Tiger Woods.

Alone.

And this is the way it's going to be for another 20 years. Mind if I play through?

Newsweek, June 2, 1997

WAIT! IT'S NOT SUPPOSED TO END THIS WAY, IS IT?

Jim Murray

I suppose Babe Ruth must have struck out some time with the bases loaded and the pennant on the line, might have popped up in the ninth inning of a World Series game.

You have to figure Michael Jordan missed from the foul line with the game tied some time in his career.

And, maybe, Willie Mays made the third out in the ninth inning of a key game some time, although I have to say I can't recall it.

Dempsey went down swinging, Arthur Ashe might have missed a key lob at match point. Nolan Ryan might have walked in the winning run at some point in his career.

It could have happened.

And I'll tell you something: If Tiger Woods is standing on a tee of a par-five 18th hole in a playoff, you've got to feel it'll come out all right. You've got to feel sorry for the other guy. For one thing, you know the first thing he's going to hear out on that fairway is "you're away!" Or, "I believe it's you."

So Billy Mayfair had the role of the foil, just the opponent in another morality play Sunday in the final round of the Nissan L.A. Open. He had managed to stay even with the great man. Now all he had to do was beat him. On a par-five. They make par-fives for Tiger Woods.

There might have been, oh, as many as 12 people in the gallery pulling for Mayfair. His mother and several others. His dogs maybe. The television networks probably wondered why he couldn't just concede so they could wrap it up and go to 60 minutes. I mean, he wasn't going to win anyway, was he?

Well, we might not know if Babe Ruth didn't call his shot. Roberto Clemente might have hit into a double-play in an extra inning, though I doubt it. Maybe Jackie Robinson got thrown out stealing against the Yanks.

And Tiger Woods can be beaten. Pass it around. Or, better yet, don't pass it around. The general public doesn't want to know. Next thing you know, someone will be telling them there's no Easter bunny.

The 1998 Nissan L.A. Open at Valencia was going along swimmingly. Tiger Woods, America's Team, if you will, had the golf course at his mercy. He had shot a 65 on Friday and was on his way to a 66 on Sunday. The rest of the field was coming apart around him. You were looking around for a Sousa march to accompany Woods into the clubhouse.

Tommy Armour double-bogeyed, Bob Estes double-bogeyed, Scott Hoch had four bogeys in nine holes. John Daly was being John Daly, Payne Stewart was just trying to keep the wheels on.

And Tiger Woods was being Tiger Woods. Birdie-birdie-birdie—six in all.

We had all seen this film before. Bring the family. Nobody could hold that Tiger.

Then there was Billy Mayfair. Now, what can I tell you about Billy Mayfair? Well, first of all, a lot of us old-timers on the tour mix him up with Billy Maxwell. They're almost the same person. Same build, same flaxen hair, almost same swing.

Billy Mayfair is built along the general lines of a bowling ball. He hits these nice, high, floating shots. He doesn't overpower a course. He's won a couple of championships, but mostly he finishes 12th. You can tell right away he's not Hogan. Tiger Woods might get beat by a Greg Norman, but not a Billy Mayfair.

He began Sunday one shot ahead of Woods, but everybody knew that wouldn't last. Still, Mayfair kept finding a way to stay in the game. Playing a group behind Woods, he almost apologetically kept abreast. Nothing fancy, just bogey-free golf.

Still, no one took it seriously. Justice would triumph. Poetic justice, at least.

Take Woods on the 18th hole in regulation. He needed a birdie, right?

Now, 18 is a 566-yard hall of horrors with the pin hanging over a sand trap. A Tiger Woods hole.

But he snaps his drive into the right rough. He takes a drop, then winds up like Ruth on a fastball. He swings from the heels. It goes into a sand trap. Frowns, all around.

Not to worry. Woods comes out of that trap with a tricky 15–20 foot putt. He makes it. Tiger always makes those.

But Mayfair comes out of a trap and makes his putt too. Playoff. Sudden death and all that.

It's O.K. Woods has never lost a playoff in the pros. And he has won three amateur championships at match play.

So, it's just victory delayed. But wait a minute! Some of us remember playoffs that were anti-history, anti-hero. Didn't Fleck beat Hogan? Casper beat Palmer? Trevino beat Nicklaus? Simpson beat Watson? Stuff happens.

They tee it up on 18 in the playoff. Mayfair hits a nice, safe, center-fairway shot. Woods tries to rip it. Once again, he's in the right rough. Once again, he's like a fighter throwing crazy rights. He tries to muscle a three-wood onto the green, which is protected on four sides by watchdog sand traps. The shot dumps in the rough.

Meanwhile, Billy Mayfair has hit a nice safe second shot. A four-iron. It's the sensible shot. He's in the fairway. He is able to spin the ball. He lands it on the green above the hole and it spins back to birdie range. Textbook way to play the hole.

Woods' shot won't stop. Out of that rough, it rolls into two-putt range.

So Woods can be beaten. Is beaten. You feel as if Jerry Rice dropped a touchdown in a corner of the end zone, Ken Griffey took a third strike with the tying run on third.

Tiger Woods is 22 years old. Billy Mayfair is 31. Maybe the day will come when he will know it's wiser to play that layup game.

I hope not. If he does that, he won't be Tiger Woods. And, hey! Babe Ruth lost the 1926 World Series when he was thrown out stealing with two outs in the bottom of the ninth inning of Game 7. If you've got to go out, it's better to go out trying. Our heroes don't play for ties.

Los Angeles Times, March 2, 1998

FALLING FOR TIGER WOODS

Erin Aubry Kaplan

My boyfriend at the time, a sometime actor and longtime caddy, did not take kindly to my new interest. He was solidly with Tiger throughout the Masters triumph — "Kicked those white boys' asses up and down the fairway!" he exulted — but quickly lost empathy when I began sighing over the latest Nike Tiger ad or gazing at a *Sports Illustrated* photo spread with a charged reverence he thought should be reserved for him. To admire Tiger as a bastion of racial uplift was OK; to consider him as anything beyond was blasphemous and unsettling. There was nothing my boyfriend could do but set about deconstructing a myth I had already made; of course he failed, and we eventually split. He took particular umbrage to the fact that a couple of girlfriends and I drove up to Palm

Springs one weekend last fall because Tiger was playing in a tournament at La Quinta. None of us had ever been to such an event before, but we were willing to do anything (which wound up including changing a flat tire and enduring snubs by tournament officials) for a glimpse of the Man. "Tiger Woods!" my ex sputtered in the end. "He's all right. He's . . . a kid. Nothing special about him."

"Beg your pardon?" I said, not bothering to conceal my sarcasm. "Nothing special?"

"Well. First of all, he looks like a whole lot of people I know. Common. Second of all, he probably won't be around that long. I know golf, and golf goes away from you. You're great one minute, a dog the next. There're a whole lot of guys been through that." He went on to detail how Tiger's ferocious swing would throw out his back, how his quick temper and penchant for winning would always undermine the patience that was much more essential to success than he yet realized. He inferred that Tiger was a lot like a million other brothers out there who, however smart and however willing, were destined to lose their way.

Not that I'm trying to establish a pattern, but I've gotten similar Tiger wariness from other black men, men for whom athletes are a no-brainer when it comes to objects of admiration. Nor do they seem to mind when the women they're close to profess an affinity for Michael Jordan, Jerry Rice, Ken Griffey Jr. But they are superstars to the point of seeming most real as video montages and marketing strategies, not people; Tiger is that rare superstar who seems unfinished, emotionally accessible, in part because golf grants him amazing space. He is a cowboy, a range rat. Rather than sharing turf with 10 other players or squeezing shoulder to shoulder on a bench, he is always alone with a vast green canvas. When he muffs a putt, he flinches for a gallery of thousands, and the world, to see. At one point in the tournament, flushed from the sun and having to hustle from green to green like so many foxholes, I was crouched directly behind him, right at his pants leg. He stood a couple of inches off, arms folded and lost in thought, tall and deeply brown and borderline skinny and, in the most extraordinary sense of the word, ordinary. My ex was right, but not in the way he thought; I could have swooned.

Close up, Tiger squirmed beneath his famous telegenic cool: He sighed, fidgeted a little, blew his nose, moved to take off his cap but thought the better of it, sighed again. In the dead spaces between strokes he didn't entirely know what to do with himself, and couldn't decide because he didn't know who or what was watching him, so he could only stand looking a little bewildered and overly solemn. The constraints of his altar-boy composure were nearly palpable, and my heart went out to him; despite having obscene amounts of money, Tiger had to be in one hell of a spot. I wanted more than anything to express my sympathy, but golf etiquette forced me into that same damn silence.

A year later Tiger is not as routinely setting the world afire (neither am I, but I'm trying) and the world is growing impatient, sometimes nastily so. Consider: He finishes in the top five in all of the tournaments he plays for the first three months of the year, fourth in the Masters, third in the rigorous British Open, and it is not good enough. A sports analyst on cable television grouses that "Tiger has shown me nothing." Oprah gets him back on the show so that he can publicly assess this slacking off. A recent item in the sports page of the *Los Angeles Times* concludes that Nike made a big mistake in sinking millions into creating a line of Tiger golf wear that is too funky for older people, too conservative for hip-hoppers — Tiger, alas, is essentially a man without a market.

The spotlight swung back to him, briefly, in the recent PGA Championship, in which he led on the first day of play with a record-setting score of 66. But other players quickly moved ahead, then eclipsed him, and though Tiger wound up finishing in the top 10, nobody would describe it as anything but a disappointment. All this doomsday is, of course, nonsense to me. Tiger still claims all the stars in my eyes and most of the space of one wall of my office cubicle. One homemade caption taped above a pensive magazine picture of him reads, OOOOOO BABY!! and elicits raised eyebrows from people unacquainted with my obsession. A glossy autographed picture sent to me from his management firm (but he signed it himself, I'm certain) is still tacked in an exalted place above my computer at home, just above postcard shots of my other muses — James Baldwin, Toni Morrison, Lorraine Hansberry, Oscar Wilde, Anton Chekhov. Bruce I long ago internalized, but that doesn't mean I am not seized with the feral, familiar pangs of what life might be, of what is left, when I hear the opening strains of "Thunder Road." Tiger and I have a long ways yet to travel.

Salon, October 1, 1998

A CLUB OF ONE;
WITH EPIC WIN, WOODS
STANDS ALONE IN SPORTS

Thomas Boswell

Now every runaway victory in sports, every demonstration of ability and superiority previously thought impossible, has a new benchmark.

Tiger Woods won the 100th U.S. Open today by the staggering total of 15 strokes, the largest margin in any major championship, breaking by two strokes the mark of Old Tom Morris in the 1862 British Open. Exhibiting imperial control of every aspect of his kingly game, Woods shot a 67 today to break the Open scoring record for most strokes under par, finishing at 12-under 272.

As the world's best players collapsed, Woods only got better with every hole. He played one course, one sport; everyone else played another. They chased him; he chased history.

The 24-year-old created a masterwork in his national championship that can stand with equal eminence beside his 12-stroke win in the Masters, another of golf's Grand Slam tournaments, in 1997. Performances such as these are the foundations upon which genuine sports legends, which surpass the dimensions of any one game, are constructed.

"I've felt tranquil . . . calm . . . peaceful all week," said Woods, who left runner-ups Ernie Els and Miguel Angel Jimenez far behind. "No matter what happened, I was able to keep my cool out there."

On a glorious, warm day along the Carmel cliffs, crowds a dozen deep followed Woods, hoping for a glimpse of a man who already had shouldered his way into comparisons with Jack Nicklaus as well as the greatest American athletes in any sport. Children carved "Tiger" signs in the sand along the Pacific beaches where Woods might see them. One fan wore a head-to-toe Tiger suit, complete with orange face paint and whiskers. Another carried a sign on Father's Day that said, "Sorry, Dad, I Had to Come See Tiger."

However, another group of fans, including former baseball commissioner Peter Ueberroth, PGA Tour Commissioner Tim Finchem and NBC President Dick Ebersol, may have had a broader perspective for appreciating Woods's amazing achievement.

"This is probably the last step in a 3 $1/2$-year process for [Woods] to join [Muhammad] Ali and [Michael] Jordan as the only athletes in the TV generation to be larger than life," said Ebersol, whose network got an extremely strong 7.5 overnight rating Saturday. "They bring in fans who have casual interest, at best, into the sport just to see them."

On one level, Woods's romp was merely a continuation of his amazing 13-month dominance of a sport that has, for more than 50 years, eluded the sole mastery of any one man, even Nicklaus. Since last June, Woods has won 15 events worldwide, including six in a row on the PGA Tour, the 1999 PGA Championship and five Tour events halfway through this season.

However, in another sense, this triumph—in overpowering style on America's most revered Open venue—broke new ground for Woods. He answered the last question about his golf stature. Could he win the one event played under conditions ideally suited to thwarting his monstrously long-hitting game? Now Woods has another facet to his game; he has whipped the five-inch rough, the rock-hard greens surrounding each hole and the slick putting surfaces that require more of a bump-and-run game and normally make the Open a humbling survival contest for the field.

Of 156 players, none could break par—except Woods, who matched the lowest round in an Open at Pebble Beach (65) on Thursday and then led wire-to-wire. Golf insiders now gladly concede that if Woods can win here—and win by 15 shots—he can win anywhere, including the windswept British Open, played next month at St. Andrews. The Old Course has several short par-4s that Woods can reach with a drive. A win there would make him the youngest winner of all four golf majors.

Every aspect of this Open served to separate Woods from every other player in his sport. He was the longest driver, averaging more than 302 yards. But he also was the most accurate iron player, leading the event in greens hit in regulation. As for putting, that may have been Woods's strongest suit.

"There comes a point when you need to make that big par putt to keep the momentum going or build on something you've already done. And I've been able to make those par putts this week. . . . For some reason, they make you feel even better than a birdie," said Woods, who has treated those 10-footer soul-testers like tap-ins.

Through the 20th century, the U.S. Open was thought to be the hardest tournament to win as well as the major title usually won by the slimmest margin. Such greats as Sam Snead and Seve Ballesteros never won it, and Arnold Palmer, Byron Nelson, Gary Player and Tom Watson only captured one Open each. Playoffs decided 31 titles; another 25 were won by one stroke.

To start a new Open millennium, Woods changed all that. Not in a generation, since Tony Jacklin won the 1970 Open by seven shots, has golf seen anything remotely akin to Woods's domination here. "The last century was mine," said four-time Open winner Nicklaus after his 44th and last Open appearance. "Tiger can have this one."

Today, he took it. Woods made par on his first nine holes and dispelled the notion that he might collapse like Greg

Norman, who held huge leads at the '96 Masters. Where Norman was foolishly aggressive that day, Woods played ultra-cautiously, using irons on several tees and aiming at the middle of greens.

What about his chance to set Open records? That did not distract Woods, as it might others of his age. Insuring his victory came first. His play here was old and wise beyond his years—just more bad news for all the superb golfers around the world who've been reduced to a Tiger entourage.

Once he had left the most treacherous seaside holes behind and turned inland, Woods unleashed 320-yard drives and made birdies at the 10th, 12th, 13th and 14th holes. Any questions?

The only one left, it seems, concerns the eventual heights Woods may reach. He has won three U.S. Junior Amateurs, three U.S. Amateurs, three major pro championships and 20 Tour events since turning pro in 1996. At the end of this day, the same thought accompanied Woods that has followed him since he putted against Bob Hope on "The Mike Douglas Show" at the age of 2, then shot 48 for nine holes at the age of 3.

How much better can he possibly get? In the past, the answer has always been the same. Just wait. And be amazed.

Washington Post, June 18, 2000

WITH THE COURSE HE'S ON, THINGS CAN ONLY GET BETTER

Thomas Boswell

In terms of job appeal, the career of pro golfer has just sunk somewhere below cannonball catching and fire-eating. Until Tiger Woods loses his gifts — which could take 20 years or more — not too many ambitious young men are going to awake every morning with the dream of becoming the best golfer who ever lived.

The job's taken. Or, probably will be within a few years, by Woods.

Fortunately, Jack Nicklaus decided to say, "That's the end," as he walked off the last green in his 44th U.S. Open on Friday. He's wise to leave the stage so his records, his memories and his legacy can stand by themselves to battle Woods. They're the only competition Tiger's got.

By the look of the demoralized generation at this 100th U.S. Open, it may take a decade to unearth a true rival. Surely Sergio Garcia — Europe's "Next Tiger" — noticed that his 299 total here wasn't quite good enough. Tiger beat him by 27. When you go back to the practice range, how do you get 27 strokes better?

"Don't give them any hope," Woods said, summarizing his Sunday strategy.

As if.

At the moment, Woods has reduced all of golf to a kind of sublime hopelessness. What he's been doing for the last 13 months is electric. TV ratings indicate the public can't get enough of Tiger's tour de force testaments to himself. But Woods may also be electrocuting the competitive spirit of every other player.

We may never, in any sport, hear the kind of concession comments that Woods's Open foes uttered. "If we get an earthquake, I might win," said Richard Zokol after posting the early lead. "He's in a league of his own. When he's putting the way he is this week, he's totally unbeatable," said John Huston. "Whatever I say is an understatement," said runner-up Ernie Els.

"For some reason, people are still doubting this guy a bit," said Rocco Mediate. "Catch him? Are you kidding me? I really think he can win 10–15 tournaments a year. He's that good."

Even Lee Janzen, who's won the Open twice and should resist any idea of Woods hegemony, said only a composite player could tackle Tiger. "Someone who can drive 300 yards every time, is smart enough to play the right shots into the greens, has the imagination to curve the ball, is strong enough to get out of the rough and holes every putt in sight," he said.

Tom Watson, however, gave the obituary for the tour. "He's changed his swing so that now he has probably the best golf swing on tour. He's probably the longest hitter. He has about the best short game. He's one of the best putters. That's why he's 10 shots ahead of the field. . . . They're all playing for second place."

Even Woods concedes, almost welcomes, the reality that he will go through periods when he doesn't win, or at least doesn't win very much. "Sometimes, you're going to go through streaks where you're just not playing well," he said after this win. "That's the way it is in golf."

Nonetheless, Tiger has won 12 of his last 21 tour events. That's twice the pace Nicklaus set in his prime. "Jack caught golf with its pants down when he came out. We've seen the same with Tiger," said Nick Price. "I feel sorry for the young guys."

Actually, he's earning it all. In American pro golf the largest margin of victory, right back to the 1924 Corpus Christi Open or any other obscure event you want to exhume, is 16 strokes. It's been done three times, but not since 1948. So, when Woods wins the U.S. Open by 15 shots at Pebble Beach, the psychological impact on his opponents is colossal.

True, Nicklaus once won a Masters by nine strokes, a PGA Championship by seven and a U.S. Open by four. So, the Golden Bear lapped a few fields in his time. He didn't just beat the Arnold Palmers and Gary Players. He squashed them all flat, too.

Nonetheless, nobody has ever separated himself from his contemporaries as Woods had by sundown Sunday beside the Pacific. As he walked up the 18th fairway, Woods told himself to enjoy the moment — a luxury he seldom allows. "All you have to do to win is stay alive," he said he told himself. "I figured that would be pretty easy since I don't have a big pot belly."

Woods could have pulled a John Daly and taken a 14 on the 18th hole and still won the Open by six shots. A 19 on 18 still would have won.

Who in any sport has opened such a gap? Michael Jordan, with his six NBA titles, had Magic Johnson with his five titles. Bill Russell had Wilt Chamberlain. Muhammad Ali had Joe Frazier. Mark McGwire has Sammy Sosa. Pedro Martinez has Randy Johnson. Joe Montana had Steve Young — on the same team.

Who has Tiger got?

David Duval needs to gain back 10 pounds just to look skinny. He's tried so hard to get into "great shape" to compete with Woods that he's almost disappeared.

Els has two U.S. Open titles and a swing like the reincarnation of Sam Snead. But he has no fire in his belly. He'd be the golfer of the year if a convention of psychiatrists got the vote. But a sane, mellow view of life ain't gonna beat Tiger.

Phil Mickelson? Colin Montgomerie? Neither of them has won so much as one major tournament.

Woods attributes his edge to his junior golf career. "I gained confidence at every level in all the tournaments I played," he said. "It teaches you something every time you win." These days, he's not letting anybody else share that learning experience.

The final twist at this Open is Woods, despite his youth, has avoided a swelled head. Asked "How great are you?" he seemed startled and said, "Aw, that's not exactly easy for me to answer . . . I let my clubs do the talking. . . . But I'll tell you this, I'm going to try to get better. When I'm 60, maybe I'll look back and see when my peak was and how long my prime lasted."

Is that a long enough view for you?

As everyone in golf has known for years, Woods has had only one real rival since childhood: Nicklaus. In that light, Woods's career may remain riveting for many years.

Nicklaus had three major wins by age 24, as Woods does now. Of course, Tiger's 25th birthday isn't until Dec. 30. So he's got two more shots this year. And he may need them. Nicklaus quickly added four more majors in his next three seasons. Woods actually has to increase his winning percentage in the majors (3 for 14) to stay even with Nicklaus. So let's not get too carried away.

Why does Woods grind so hard when he's already won by a ridiculous margin? Because he's always preparing for his next win in his long pursuit of the Bear. Woods doesn't just win. He tries to imprint on the mind of every opponent that resistance is useless. The military calls the tactic "overwhelming force." You paralyze the enemy to the point where he doesn't even try to fire back.

This past week at the U.S. Open, Tiger Woods showed his skill and his implacable tranquil ability to stay focused for four days. But he also showed his knack for psychological warfare as well. Not one player out of 155 here had the stomach to raise a serious challenge to Woods at any point in this Open. In a sense, Woods won without a single shot being fired in retaliation.

That, too, is part of Woods's grand plan. And it's working.

Washington Post, June 19, 2000

TIGER'S TRIUMPH:
DRAMA-FREE, BUT MUST-SEE TV

Tony Kornheiser

So now we see what perfection looks like.

It's young, square-shouldered and determined. And it wears red on Sunday.

This is not the title of a slasher film, but I know what you did last weekend.

You watched Tiger.

Everybody did.

In the living rooms, the dens, the bars, in the airport lounges, all the TVs were tuned in to Tiger. In the mall, where the electronic stores have hundreds of TVs on display, they were all tuned in to Tiger. Tiger drew the highest

TV ratings the U.S. Open has ever had. He's the reason people hit the "On" button and kept the TV on until his very last shot. He's the one who makes the needle move.

If you were one of the lucky 32,500 folks at Pebble Beach over the weekend, bless you. But for the rest of us, the only way to see Tiger was on TV.

Counting six holes of the second round that carried over into Saturday because of fog on Friday, Tiger played 42 holes on the weekend. I figure I saw 41 of them. Given the fact that there were 20 hours of coverage, I had to be in the bathroom for a few minutes, so I probably missed one of Tiger's pitching wedges from 140 yards out. (Though I sure didn't miss his drive into the water on 18 on Saturday morning when he dropped the F-bomb! I was so stunned to hear that on TV, and I had so much empathy for his doomed shot, I actually applauded in my den.)

The point is: I planned my weekend around watching Tiger. I played golf early Sunday so I could be back in time to see Tiger tee off. Me and about 60 million other Americans.

And the thing of it is, we did it without expecting any drama whatsoever. Oh, sure, there was a fleeting conversation about the hopeful possibility that Ernie Els would string a few birdies together at the start of Sunday's round so Tiger might feel a breeze on the back of his neck. But nobody believed Els would come within eight shots of him. I can't say I thought Tiger would win by 15, like he did. But I knew it wasn't a horse race. There was nobody else out there. It was all Tiger. Padraig Harrington, indeed.

This is a rarity in sports, where we're always looking for something close, some decisive act at the end of a game— a Hail Mary pass to the end zone on fourth down; a three-pointer at the buzzer; a play at the plate in the bottom of the ninth.

We weren't looking for that. We were looking for Tiger. You can't take your eyes off him.

Sports aren't supposed to sustain long days on TV with only one person on stage. This is a golf tournament, not a conquest of Everest. Usually, rivalries make events compelling: Magic and Bird; Wilt and Russell; Borg and McEnroe; Evert and Navratilova.

Yet it didn't matter that Tiger was lapping the field. It reminded me of Secretariat in the 1973 Belmont Stakes. When Secretariat was nearing the finish line, TV had to pan all the way back to the far turn to see the other horses. The gap was numbing. I still think fondly of Secretariat's amazing performance as one of the most thrilling sports events I've ever seen. For obvious reasons, so was this. All weekend long there was one house rule: "If somebody calls, tell them I'll call back after the Open."

But who would call, except to talk about Tiger? About the astonishing length Tiger gets off the tee. About how preposterously close he sticks it from the bunker. About the way he scoops a wedge out of deep spinach 120 yards out, and spins it to eight feet, when nobody else could even get it to the green. How many times did we hear one of the TV guys say, "It's a terrible lie, a virtually impossible shot. But maybe I should say it would be virtually impossible for any-body but Tiger"?

Tiger is the only guy out there now who I'd change dinner plans to watch. I'm already looking forward to seeing him overpower the Old Course at St. Andrews in the British Open. With the time difference I'll be able to make breakfast plans around him.

Tiger isn't the only person I've felt this way about. As a kid there was Koufax and Oscar. In 30 years as a sports-writer there have been others: Magic Johnson, Carl Lewis, Dr. J, Joe Montana, Nolan Ryan, Ali and Tyson. Michael Jordan, of course. But the list is small. Tiger is in the rare company of athletes who are so riveting that you watch them for the possibility that at any time they might do something so majestic it gives you goose bumps. That's why when people make sports movies they write in Big Bang endings, like Robert Redford walloping a homer into the light tower in "The Natural." Because sports are supposed to be magic.

People say Tiger is great because his father put a golf club in his hands when he was 2 years old. That's ridiculous. There have been plenty of parents who put a paint brush in their children's hands at 2 years old, and there's still only one Monet.

There is genius, and who knows where it comes from?

It's been 15 years since Paul Simon wrote the "Grace-land" album. In it there's the line, "Every generation throws a hero up the pop charts." We're always looking for The Next One. And there always is A Next One.

There would never be another Babe Ruth, but now there is Mark McGwire. There would never be another Sandy Koufax, but now there is Pedro Martinez. There would never be another Wilt Chamberlain, but now there is Shaquille O'Neal.

People say there will never be another Michael Jordan.

But there already is.

He's playing golf.

Washington Post, June 20, 2000

A GENIUS COMFORTABLE WITH HIS GIFTS; ST. ANDREWS BOWS TO THE GREAT TIGER

Hugh McIllvanney

Tiger Woods has a talent so remarkable that we might expect him to be almost as over-awed by it as the rest of us are.

But no genius of sport ever gave the impression of being more comfortable with his gifts than the 24-year-old who is using the most celebrated stretch of holes in golf to redraw the boundaries of what can be achieved in the game. He wears greatness like a familiar sweater.

Nothing about his performance at St. Andrews over the past three days has been more admirable than his recognition that even abilities which are close to supernatural must be applied with practicality. The balance between inspiration and pragmatism has been nearly flawless. His imagination has soared at times but his feet have stayed planted on the sun-dried turf of the Fife littoral. Self-indulgence has not been allowed to show its face. You don't keep bogeys off your card as successfully as he has done at the Old Course if giving rein to flights of fancy. We have been watching a man at work. When necessary, Mozart has put on the dungarees.

Woods's awareness of how special he has become is unmistakable. But if he is always willing to embrace the extravagant possibilities of his shot-making, he is rarely seduced into expensive miscalculation of the percentages. That increasing discipline, and the quality of mind he brings to the deployment of his unique physical resources, leave us with no option but to assume that the kind of hardship he is inflicting on his competitors this weekend is part of a pattern he is liable to maintain for years to come. Today won't produce anything resembling the winning margin of 15 strokes he had in the US Open at Pebble Beach (it was the biggest recorded since the launching of major championships back in the 19th century) but the chances of any of his rivals catching him are negligible.

Though he has won plenty of tournaments by charging from behind, he has an intelligent preference for the role of front-runner. When asked on Friday night about the pressures of having the lead, he employed a blast of common sense to demonstrate that only the eccentric would be reluctant to go ahead of the field early: "I've always enjoyed being in the lead. When you're there, if you make a mistake it is not as costly as it is when you are behind. You might run into a couple of bogeys and still not do too much damage. You are under more pressure when you are chasing. Then you are forced to play well. If you get a couple of bogeys, you could be out of the tournament."

According to the bookmakers, Woods had already dumped the rest of the world's golfing elite out of contention at the midway point of the 129th Open. By then his original odds of 9–4 against, which had been widely regarded as outrageously short, had shrunk to an unbackable price of 5–1 on, and the layers had started making a separate book that did not involve him at all. They had decided that his pursuers were competing for second place.

Anybody who questioned the logic of the betting firms' assumptions had not been paying attention to the recent statistics of the phenomenon's career. Before arriving in Scotland, he had won 15 of the previous 28 tournaments he had entered, a strike rate calculated to deepen the collective sense of inferiority that has been engulfing those who go out to earn their living alongside him. And still gloomier portents for his fellow professionals are buried in more obscure sets of figures. It is widely imagined that he must have been at a personal zenith when he turned that US Open into a solo event, but the truth is that some of his statistics were slightly out of tune with a 15-shot victory.

For example, his success in hitting fairways only tied him for 14th in the ratings at Pebble Beach and in putting he was tied for sixth. Nick Faldo, who finished seventh, had six fewer putts and Colin Montgomerie, who shared 46th position, landed on five more fairways. Those comparisons were utterly irrelevant that weekend but, as is emphasised by Tom Callahan, a leading American golf journalist who has made a particular study of Woods, they do challenge the notion that he was as close to perfection as he is ever likely to be.

"I'm sure we haven't seen anything like the limits of what Tiger can do," said Callahan. "I can envisage him going into a tournament, getting everything to come together throughout the four days and shooting frightening numbers, maybe four rounds of about 61.

"With him, exaggerating his potential is less of a danger than under estimating it. He has already shown how crazy it was to suggest, as many did not long ago, that it would be impossible for any individual to be completely dominant in modern golf. And nobody can credit the standards he sets to improvements in equipment. Compared with others on the Tour, he uses pretty old-fashioned clubs. The fact is he has more talent than anybody else who ever played the game. I think he is greater than Nicklaus, Hogan, any of the giants of the past, and I believe his performances will prove it."

When missing a short putt caused Woods to drop a shot on the second green yesterday, it was the first time he had endured that indignity in major championship play since the 10th hole at Pebble Beach in the third round of the American Open, a run of 63 holes at par or better. With several players farther out on the course capitalising on weather conditions that continued to favour low scoring, there was a sudden threat to his breathing space at the top of the leaderboard. But punters who had wagered on him were unlikely to take fright, since temperament has become one of his key weapons. The aberration scarcely qualified as a hiccup. He birdied the third hole to go back to his overnight score of 11 under par, and by the finish he was 16-under and six shots clear.

There is fire burning not far from the surface and it flares briefly now and then in flourishes of temper, when he slaps his putter to the ground, or snarls an expletive at himself. Generally, however, his demeanour at St Andrews has seemed to reflect the conviction that, if he goes on delivering his best, both the ancient links and his human opposition will have to yield. Patience has been one of his most impressive characteristics and it was exemplified at the fifth tee during his second round, when the worst congestion of the tournament obliged him to wait 36 minutes before he could use his driver for the first time that day. He was so far from being disconcerted that he teased a birdie out of that difficult par five with an approach putt of stunning delicacy from far down the steep slope of fairway that falls away from the front of the green.

While waiting among a clutch of former Open champions to gain access to the fifth tee, Woods had been the essence of relaxation. He ate a snack bar and chatted amiably to his playing partners, Nick Price and David Gossett, the US amateur champion, and to his close friend and Florida neighbour Mark O'Meara. Although he acknowledged afterwards that he had been worried about staying loose through that disruptive delay, he was plainly no more affected by it at the time than any of the veterans around him.

He was sufficiently free of tension to converse about subjects far removed from the urgent concerns of the moment. At his end-of-round press conference he stressed the anxiety he had felt about losing his rhythm while hanging around, but as he stretched out on the grassy mounds between the fourth green and the next tee, he might have been exchanging stories in his back garden. At one point he was telling the younger Gossett about how much hounding from the media his fame has brought him. He explained that it had reached an especially troublesome pitch when he was bidding to win seven tournaments in a row and had attracted the full heat of the tabloid press's attention.

"One of the things they did to try to get into my room was that they made out there was a medical emergency," Woods said. "One time they were suggesting there was something seriously wrong with my mom."

Soon that strange little suspension of the drama of the Open was over and he was back at the task of fashioning the round of 66 that was to thrust him three shots in front at half-way and invite the bookies and every other rational judge to declare the contest all but over. As he surged aggressively into the back nine yesterday, it was a relief to see that the man ranked No. 2 in the world, David Duval, had negotiated the Old Course in 66 strokes and confirmed that he is recovering the form which carried him to the top of the rankings less than two years ago. Ernie Els was also prominent on the leader board but, in fact, nobody was close enough to promise a competitive Sunday. Woods should make stately progress today towards the distinction of being the youngest golfer to have won all four major championships.

The long-term hope must be that players as outstanding as Els and Duval will not have their spirits broken by the evidence of Woods's absolute supremacy that is constantly thrust at them. There have been worrying signs of late that their expectations of themselves could be reduced by repeated batterings. American sports observers have been reminded of the devastation perpetrated on a rival psyche by another towering talent—and one that could not even speak. Secretariat was a thoroughbred marvel of the 1970s, winner of the Triple Crown of US Classics. The horse that suffered most from Secretariat's greatness was Sham, who finished just two-and-a-half lengths behind him in both the Kentucky Derby and the Preakness. In the third Classic, the Belmont Stakes, Sham's heart cracked and he trailed in dead last, 45 lengths adrift of his torturer.

Some serious watchers of golf fear that Tiger Woods could make every other professional in the game feel a bit like Sham.

Times of London, July 7, 2000

THE GREATEST

James Lawton

As natural as Pele. As tough as
Bradman. As pretty as Ali. As clean as Lewis. As prolific as
Sampras. At only 24, Tiger Woods may already be the most
phenomenal sportsman of all time

The proposition is stunning, outrageous in its offence
against some of the classic definitions of ultimate achievement in any walk of life. But then genius makes it owns
rules, sets its own deadlines, and so this morning no one
can dispute the possibility that, at 24 years of age, Tiger
Woods is already well on the way to proving himself the
greatest sportsman who ever lived.

Some, no doubt, will insist the title will always be elusive. How, they will ask, can you precisely compare the nas-
cent glory of Woods, who on Sunday night on the Valhalla

course in Kentucky became only the second golfer in history to win three major titles in one year, with Muhammad Ali's extraordinary journey into the world's consciousness, or Don Bradman's phenomenal, career-long mastery of the art of batsmanship, or the unchallenged ascendancy of Pele on the football field?

In some ways you can't. No one will ever try to tear off the Tiger's head as he lines up one of those heart-stopping putts – as such ferocious customers as Sonny Liston, Joe Frazier and George Foreman did to Ali. No one will devise a check on Woods's route to the mountain top that involves a calculated attempt to do him serious injury – as the English tourists under Douglas Jardine did to the young Bradman in the notorious "body-line" series. Half a football team will not be designated the role of crippling Woods – as Brazil's rivals did to Pele in the 1966 World Cup.

No, the worst they can do to Woods is make him play to the very limits of his ability and his temperament, as Bob May, a 31-year-old journeyman golfer from Southern California, did so unforgettably at Valhalla on Sunday. But then golf will always be a game of the mind as much as the body, and all the available evidence is that, at a remarkably tender age, the Tiger's mind is as tough as tungsten.

It is three years since Woods first invaded the imagination of the sporting world by winning the Masters by the shattering margin of 12 strokes and with a record score of 18-under par. Jack Nicklaus never did anything quite like that – and until this year of Tiger, this annexation of an entire sport by one young, beautifully balanced and phenomenally composed young man, Nicklaus was golf's rock-solid entry for the mythic title of the world's greatest sportsman. Nicklaus, the Golden Bear of Ohio, defined the best values of the game. He surpassed the power of the beloved Arnie Palmer, who was freely acknowledged as the father of modern golf; he amassed a mountain of majors – 18 of them – a mark which everyone said would stand for ever.

Once, on a deserted practice range in Ohio, Nicklaus told me of his agony at the possibility that he was losing his game. He talked of his pain that his father, who had built braziers on frozen tees and converted the basement of the family house into a driving range against the rigours of the mid-West winter, had died at a time when Jack's golf seemed to be ebbing. He had only the fireflies for company as he toiled into the night, endlessly hitting the golf ball and cursing: "Goddamit, how can I hit so it so well and yet no longer win a tournament?" That was in 1979.

Seven years later he won his sixth green jacket at the Masters in Augusta, and just two years ago he made that fabled place of golf stand still with the possibility that he might just win it again.

Such is the man who last weekend in Valhalla, in scenes of high emotion, passed on the torch to his successor. Nicklaus and Woods played together for the first two days of the PGA tournament, and for golf aficionados there were also moments of unbearable poignancy. None compared with the moment of Nicklaus's "blessing." It came when Tiger

Woods drilled one of his customised long putts, a thing of snaking beauty and perfect control. Jack Nicklaus smiled paternally, winked broadly at Woods and gave the thumbs-up sign. No emperor ever surrendered his throne with such grace – or warmth.

"Tiger," said Nicklaus later, "is playing so well it is impossible to imagine he could be doing anything better. He has done everything right. He is in control of everything. Conditions change . . . and I have to say that, so far, Tiger has yet to be as seriously challenged. But you see him play, you spend a little time in his company, and you have to believe he will be equal to anything that is put before him. He is an amazing young man."

Amazing in his ability, not least, to live with the sheer weight of the fame that has accumulated so quickly, so relentlessly. On Sunday, America tuned into the phenomenon of Woods, but it would be idle to pretend that a nation still marked by racism did so without ambivalence. One bar-room joke hints at the shock of seeing a young black man marching through the open doors of America's country clubs. "What were you looking at 40 years ago when a bunch of white men were chasing a single black?" Answer: the Ku Klux Klan. "What are looking at today?" Answer: a major golf tournament.

Not the least of Woods's achievements is his effortless handling of the race issue. Two years ago, a fellow pro, former Masters winner Fuzzy Zoeller, made what were considered to be tasteless remarks about the likely menu Woods would decree at the annual champions' dinner at Augusta. Zoeller mentioned "greens and chitlings," the food of poor blacks. Woods, who grew up in middle-class Southern California, was offended on the basis that race was irrelevant to his situation. He demanded, and received, an apology – and moved on, a child not of one section of American society but of the wide sporting world.

Woods's status as the man golf is now obliged to hold up against the titans of other sports is hard to challenge on any point of style or temperament or dedication. Or statistics. In any straight comparison with the 24-year-old Nicklaus, he wins in a canter. At 24, Nicklaus had tour earnings of $1.6m, a figure adjusted for inflation; Woods has won $17m. Nicklaus had won three majors; Woods has won four, and three of them by numbing margins. On the tour, Nicklaus had picked up 12 tournament wins; Woods has 21. Nicklaus had a scoring average of 69.96; Woods is two strokes better at 67.77. The list is long, and in every category Woods has superior figures, even in their earliest recorded scores over nine holes. At 10 years old, Nicklaus shot a 51; at three, Woods was three shots better.

Behind these statistics is a will that is already spoken of with awe. Nick Faldo, by far Britain's most successful modern golfer, with five big victories, provoked some chilly mirth at St Andrews last month, when Woods turned the great tournament into a formal procession: "It is as though Tiger has invented a new game. Am I upset? Not all." He then threw his golf cap to the ground.

Woods's coach, Butch Harmon, says: "When Tiger spots a weakness in his game he simply works – and I really mean works – on it. His putting is the best example. He has slaved at this putting. You know the scary part? He's only at about 75 per cent of what he's capable of."

It's not only the game that has been changed by Woods. Colin Montgomerie, the pride of Europe for seven years but still pursuing his first major, has slimmed down by 20 lbs. David Duval, ranked second in the world, has started an exercise and weight-training routine after hearing that the Tiger has added 20 lbs. of muscle. But they trail in the wake of Woods. Recently Woods reflected on a conversation with Sam Snead. Slammin' Sam told him that in his day players thought nothing of "partying" most of the night, then taking a hangover on to the course. Woods pinched his lips: "I'm afraid that doesn't work anymore."

What works so supremely well is an unparalleled willingness to master every aspect of the game. Does this make Tiger Woods the greatest sportsman of all time? Can he carry the ground owned by the sublimely gifted and spirited Ali? Can he go along the long road of perfection trod by Bradman? Can he find the sheer competitive stamina which drove Carl Lewis to gold in four Olympics? Perhaps it is too early to say, maybe there will never be a day when such a claim can be made on behalf of a single sportsman. But something can be said, as confidently as Woods addresses the golf ball on a tortuous, sloping green with everything to win and lose. It is that no one has ever realised so perfectly, so quickly, all the talent he has been given.

No one has ever wanted it more, or been so willing to explore everything within himself in order to get it. This means he has a chance. One provided by the gods.

Independent, August 22, 2000

BROKEN RECORD: TIGER WOODS DOES IT AGAIN FOR A CAREER GRAND SLAM AT 24

Dan Jenkins

Tiger Woods provided a lot of memories from the British Open at St. Andrews—like the variety of ways in which he turned the Old Course into a plate of mince, neeps and tatties—but a classic remark of his, uttered in the heat of battle, lives on.

There was this moment in Saturday's third round when he was at the 14th hole, the 581-yard par 5, building a six-shot lead through 54 holes, going for his fifth birdie in seven holes, intent on letting everybody know they'd better stop jacking with him on the leader boards.

What he did was, he lashed a 3-wood shot with full force, a shot he hoped would reach the green in two and give him an eagle putt and surely a two-putt birdie. It was only an instant after he swung that you knew by his expression that he liked it. Knew he'd clubfaced it, stung it.

You had to imagine that Steve Williams, his caddie, had just said something to him on the order of "show me that 290-yard, 3-wood draw of yours." And that's when Tiger, knowing he'd pured it, with the ball only halfway home, knifing through the air, casually said to Steve:

"That the one you're talking about?"

Not cocky, just confident. The most self-assured player in the game. Another defining moment in the life of the game's greatest golfer. Then, of course, he goes out in Sunday's final round and more or less hits the same shot again at the 14th, one of the many controlled shots he hit to shower the premises with almost as many records as there were people, which was a record in itself. More than 230,000 attended this Open during the week, and another curious record is that five of them decided to shed their clothes, hop over the ropes and run around the golf course naked before being led away by the local constabulary—the five-streaker Open.

If you want to compare Tiger Woods with Jack Nicklaus, consider his accomplishments with those of Jack at the same age of 24: Tiger now has seven majors. Jack had five. Tiger has 21 PGA Tour victories. Jack had 12. Tiger has 27 world victories. Jack had 15. Tiger has $17 million in career prize money. Jack had $275,000. Heck, Tiger's caddie even made $700,000 last year, which would have put him in the top 60 money-winners if he'd bothered to take a divot somewhere.

You want to hear about birdies and bogeys, go somewhere else. When it seemed a lock that the guy who's surely the most famous athlete in the world today was going to win this British Open, something took place that you'd normally expect to happen around Buckingham Palace. Tiger's handlers and some officials of the R&A planned for the coronation.

A mole supplied me with a peek at the schedule. Which was:

6:45—Tiger records his score. 6:57—Tiger supplies quick quotes for pool reporter. 7:00—Tiger grants two-minute interviews to ABC, BBC and Radio 5. 7:06—Prize giving. 7:12—Tiger does photo ops at prize table. 7:20 to 8:00— Tiger does mass interview in press tent. 8:10—Tiger attends champagne reception in R&A Committee Tent. 8:30— Tiger grants three-minute interview to ESPN, CNN and maybe somebody else.

Not included: Tiger goes out to look for bodies that were pushed into the Swilcan Burn as he marched up the final fairway. Some, like David Duval, who was last seen taking four shots to get out of the Road Bunker, have still not been recovered.

For several days before the 2000 British Open began there was nothing but talk in the periodicals about Tiger Woods completing the career Grand Slam. Joining Jack Nicklaus, Ben Hogan, Gary Player and Gene Sarazen, the

174 / Broken Record

only ones who'd done it, and doing it at a younger age. As everyone on the globe was aware—everyone, perhaps, except a tourist who missed the last bus out of the Congo—Tiger had already collected a Masters, PGA, and U.S. Open in his still-brief pro life.

But the discussion was all wrong. Enter the D.H., your friendly neighborhood Designated Historian.

Walter Hagen, Tommy Armour and Jim Barnes did the pro slam long before any of those other immortals. Given the fact that the Western Open was inarguably a major before the Masters came along, and even continued to be regarded as a major for a few years after that by the equipment and apparel folk, who gave bonuses for winning it, the accomplishments of Hagen, Armour and Barnes must be counted, please.

When Hagen won the 1922 British Open at Sandwich, he completed the professional Slam, for he had already captured the 1914 and 1919 U.S. Opens, the 1916 Western, and the 1921 PGA. Of course, nobody thought to credit The Haig with such a feat back then. Same for Armour, who won the 1927 U.S. Open, 1929 Western, 1930 PGA and 1931 British Open. And Long Jim Barnes completed it after he won the British Open at Prestwick in 1925. He had already taken the Western Opens of 1914, 1917, and 1919 as well as the first two PGAs in 1916 and 1919, and the U. S. Open of 1921. Seven majors, yet he must be the most obscure golf immortal ever with today's audience.

Speaking of immortals, Jack Nicklaus was probably playing his last British Open at St. Andrews this July, and received standing ovations each time he strode up a fairway and walked onto a green for the 36 holes he played.

In a moving moment on Friday, he paused atop the Swilcan Bridge on the 18th to wave goodbye to what seemed like the town's entire population.

Jack did play in that four-hole pre-tournament event earlier on Wednesday for the past champions. There are 27 living past holders of the claret jug, and 22 of them showed up, including 88-year-old Sam Snead, who still has his sense of the humor. Never a big fan of courses on the olde sod, Sam glanced at the moonscape of St. Andrews and said the same thing he'd said on his last visit, when he won in '46.

"This looks like a place where there used to be a golf course," he grinned.

The Champions Challenge also saw Ian Baker-Finch, the '91 winner at Birkdale, set some kind of record when his drive from the first hole soared O.B. to the right over the huge grandstand, taking dead aim on the North Sea. It was back in the '95 Open at St. Andrews that he had hooked it out-of-bounds to the left, into the intersection of the Links Road and Granny Clark's Wynd. Thus, he became the first man ever to hit his drive out-of-bounds on both sides of the widest fairway in all of golf.

Intolerably absent from that nostalgic shindig, by the way, was Arnold Palmer. What, he had a more important endorsement meeting?

The Open started amid stupid weather. That's what people who'd been in Scotland for a few days called it. Sunny and warm again. The way it had been for days and would continue to be almost throughout the tournament. Cashmere dealers out of business. Shirtless spectators sprawled on the ground and picnicking in the grandstands. No wonder there were so many streakers.

With the hard and slick-shaved fairways and the lack of any true wind, St. Andrews was disarmed, and more than 50 guys pounced on it to break par of 72 in the first round. There were three or four par–4 holes that could be driven from the tee, and something like 14 holes in all where the second shot was no more than 100 yards.

The only reason nobody shot lower than Ernie Els' leading 66 is because it was a major, after all. Tiger's 67 was so effortless it was almost laughable. He played the first eight holes in even par when all the Notah Begays in town seemed to be shooting them in four under, but he looked unconcerned.

As he said later: "Any time I can par the first eight holes in a major, I won't complain."

Naturally not. He knew he would eventually grab some birdies, and most likely hit one of those shots no other human can hit, and, all in all, finish in the lead or near the lead on a course where par is 68 for him.

Every day was completely his, regardless of what anyone might do before he played or after he finished. In the first two rounds of any British Open, they play golf for 15 hours, from 7 a.m. till almost 10 p.m. Els didn't finish his first round until Tiger had been done for five hours and most civilized people were having dinner.

In all those 15 hours, though, there was only one shot worth remembering—the 60-degree wedge Tiger hit at the 17th, the Road Hole, the world's toughest par 4. After pulling his drive deep in the vegetation left of the fairway, Tiger launched a shot to the front of the green that he alone can hit. A slashing iron that lifted the ball out of the knee-deep brush and moved it 160 yards. It was a swing so violent, he wound up on only one leg, and stumbling.

"A shot like that," he explained, "you have to open the face wide open and hold on tight and get your right hand into it as much as your left. It's not the lie that can stop the clubhead, it's the grass that can stop the shaft."

As amazing as anything was that Tiger had laughed and done a high-five with his caddie even before he hit the shot.

Were they celebrating the discovery of a decent lie? "No, we were just telling jokes," Tiger related.

Probably laughing about the usual Designated Lurkers that would contaminate the leader board. Or the Hagen, Armour and Barnes thing.

Actually, there was another memorable shot, provided by Notah Begay in the course of making a triple at the 17th. He went into the hole seven under and leading the Open, but he almost didn't finish it. His drive put him in the same high rough that Tiger found. Begay's first wedge went only 20 feet and was still in the weeds. His second wedge then shot so far to the left and beyond the green that it wound up in a bend of the Swilcan Burn that nobody even knew existed. It was as if he was trying to reach the Frenchman's creek at Carnoustie but didn't have enough club. He then climbed down into the burn and splashed the ball out, back onto the golf course, and took three more from there. A rare thing indeed to see someone hitting out of the narrow burn, a feat that naturally earned Begay this headline in one of the tabloids the next day: "The have-a-go Navajo." Of course, he never would have climbed into the hazard if he'd known "Swilcan" is Scottish for "sewage." In any case, his tournament more or less ended there, after he, well, more or less "Van de Velded it" at the Road Hole.

After playing himself into the championship on Friday, at least for a while, Fred Couples uttered one of the best quotes of his relatively quoteless career when he said: "I'm playing as well as I've ever played, except for the years I played better."

But Tiger's 66, a score that nobody would better all week, looked even more effortless than his first-round 67. On a course where he can normally expect to have four putts for eagles, two on par 5s and two on drivable par 4s, he made only one unwise decision during his six-under round. Again, it came at the 17th. He went for the flag with a high short iron after a perfect drive, and the ball raced across the hard putting surface and down the slope and might have been expected to wind up on the tarmac or up against the old stone wall. But no. The ball came to rest on a narrow clump of grass. He then jammed a pitch into the protective bank beyond the pin, then put the 10-foot par putt right in the throat. Thus, he turned a possible tragedy into another ho-hum 4 on the card.

Tiger's third-round 67 was sort of terrifying from the standpoint of what it could have been. Like a 63. After all, he three-putted a trio of greens and failed to birdie the gimme-birdie fifth.

His pursuers shouldn't have made him mad, is what it came down to, by creeping up on him on the leader board at one point. And nothing makes Tiger turn up the volume more than suffering some slight form of disappointment, like his three-putt at the second hole, stumbling to his first bogey in a major in 64 holes, going all the way back to the 10th at Pebble Beach in the third round of the U.S. Open. Stunned at this lapse, Tiger then played the remaining 16 holes in six under, and in a strategic seven-hole stretch, from the eighth through the 14th, he ripped off a mere five birdies.

Also, you have to marvel at how he talks about details. "I'm rolling my putts really well," he said. OK, but don't everybody's putts roll?

"I mean, mine really hug the ground," he elaborated.

There were those who tried to make a run at Tiger in the last round, but they were only kidding themselves. Woods was content to play defensively for a while, then, on the way to his closing 69 and the incredible 19-under total of 269, he slammed in the birdies at 10, 12, and 14 that removed any doubt.

The whole thing actually ended in a comedy with David Duval, his main challenger during most of the day, floundering to an 8 at the Road Hole, and Ernie Els, the Big Easy, becoming this year's Official Runner-up. Three majors, three seconds—surely another record.

Tiger only dropped three shots to par all week, largely by avoiding every one of those treacherous pot bunkers that are named after obscure old Scots or their body parts and are strewn across the links. Tiger's 19-under-par total has never been matched by anyone in any major. And he won by eight strokes—only Young Tom Morris and Old Tom Morris have won an Open by more, back in the days when mince, neeps and tatties were popular.

That means also he now holds the scoring records in three majors: 18 under at the Masters (winning by a record 12 strokes), 12 under in the U.S. Open (winning by a record 15 strokes), and that slam dunk he just made in the British Open.

There's nothing anyone can do about Tiger Woods but look at his game and swoon. You can't name a player today who does any one thing better than Tiger. OK, Jose Maria Olazabal might be better out of bunkers, but it's doubtful, and Phil Mickelson might have a better flop shot, but it's doubtful. Besides that, it's nitpicking. In any other aspect of the game, he's so dominant it's falling-down funny. He gets up in the morning and outdresses everyone, then it's a clean sweep from there.

Golf Digest, September 2000

ONE WRITER'S TIGER WOODS PROBLEM

Robert Lipsyte

In today's session, Doctor, I would like to deal with my Eldrick Tiger Woods problem. So many shrinks are lining up to play catch with Chuck Knoblauch, hiding from discussions of Darryl Strawberry, finding Freud in Nascar and gold in performance enhancement, that I'm sure someone, if not you, can help me.

I feel I am supposed to love Tiger Woods, and I need to know why I don't.

Sure, I enjoy watching him play, whale away or delicately putt, but he doesn't get under my skin the way Mickey or Muhammad or Michael did. Although my boosters and rippers on thelipsite@aol.com have been curiously and gratifyingly silent on the issue, I sense they feel disappointed by my lack of connection to a young man both Nike and Disney seem to think is the evolutionary step beyond Michael Jordan—the multicult sporting ideal, a role model for children, adults and global corporations. The news media, when they sense the need to temper their fawning Tigermania, will mildly suggest that he isn't Bobby Jones—yet. We'll get to my Bobby Jones problem. I even have a Tiger Woods repressed memory. Almost 10 years ago, on a public course in Los Angeles, a middle-age black golfer took me aside to say I was covering the wrong story. I was enchanted with an attempt by the teaching division of the Ladies Professional Golf Association to introduce underprivileged girls and boys to the game. The teaching pros thought it would not only enhance the kids' self-esteem but it would also introduce them to a world they needed to become part of. It seemed a pragmatic use of a sport that is still remarkably exclusionary while important as a business tool (despite, or because of, its white male suburban base.)

The black golfer said I should be tracking down a 15-year-old phenom who would soon overwhelm the game. The key to his success, the man said, was the furious drive of his father, a former Army colonel. The defining moment had come when the boy was 5 or 6, and Dad, in civvies, took him to a military course. Two white admirals spotted the prodigy and said, "That's some golfer you've got there, sergeant."

By assuming he was an enlisted man because of his color, the black golfer told me, the admirals had nailed Dad's determination to send his little tiger out to dominate the world. Maybe my Tiger problem is a defense against having missed the story. And maybe it's just a contrarian quirk. He is being shoved down my throat. Even that self-consciously stylized fist pump looks as if it is describing a Nike swoosh. (And yet, there he is introducing young kids to his game, just like those lady pros.)

As with Michael, there is no denying Tiger's will not only to win but to dominate crushingly. (Could this be an issue? Is there a manhood thing I'm missing?) The great champions will step on your face if that's what it takes to win. The supernatural champions, add Dale Earnhardt, seem to need to step on your face to stay in the game.

Supernatural, of course, may be the word here (the golfer Tom Watson used it to describe Tiger). Four years ago, after Earl Woods dubbed his boy the Chosen One, a Nashville radio talk show host (since fired), John Ziegler, created the erratically funny Web site TigerWoodsisGod.com. Raised as a Roman Catholic, Ziegler says he became disenchanted first with the Bible, then organized religion. Then he found golf.

He writes on his Web site: "I found no feeling that gave me a sense of order in the universe like that of a crisply struck golf shot (later in life I would learn that seeing certain women naked comes quite close)."

And later writes: "To me, if Tiger Woods is NOT God, he is at least a human lab experiment to determine the potential of our species."

Attempts to humanize Woods have usually been quickly squelched. In his classic GQ profile in 1997, Charles P. Pierce quoted Woods, then 21, telling mildly racist and sexist jokes. First, Pierce was accused of misquoting Woods. When that didn't fly, it was spun that Woods was trying to relax a film crew during a commercial shoot. Right. We know how awed those crews are by child golfers.

The Bobby Jones factor. Ziegler's irreverent comparisons of Jesus and Tiger become high satire alongside golf traditionalists' protection of Bobby Jones, an amateur whose four major victories came in the same calendar year, 1930.

Jones has been promoted as the saint of the links, this irascible Confederate princeling whose elistist and racist upbringing helped create that bastion of bigotry, the Augusta National Golf Club, and its absurdly cosseted premier event, the Masters, with its green straitjacket.

Jones's worshipers should be grateful. The coming of Eldrick the Great, who gracefully refuses to play any of his race cards, relieves Bobby and his good old boys of any retroactive guilt: how bad could they have been if golf is so ready to accept a colored fellow, even if he is arguably the greatest golfer of all time?

So why can't I love Tiger? What's wrong with me, Doctor?

"Beats me."

New York Times, April 22, 2001

TIGER TIME: THE WONDER OF AN AMERICAN HERO

Jay Nordlinger

Sometime last season, I e-mailed a friend of mine, an ex-pro golfer and a keen student of the game. "Are we ready to concede that Tiger is the best ever?" I asked. His answer was slightly ambiguous; I couldn't tell whether he was being sincere or sarcastic. So I asked for a clarification. "Oh, let me be perfectly clear," he replied. "Nicklaus in his heyday couldn't carry Tiger's clubs. Really."

Now, my friend and I were Nicklaus worshipers from way back—we still are. When it comes to Nicklaus, we are dangerously close to violating the First Commandment. So acknowledging the truth about Tiger came hard. Jack

Nicklaus—this is gospel in golf—dominated his sport as no other athlete ever dominated any sport. I once began a piece about Nicklaus roughly this way: Boxing folks can talk about Louis versus Ali; baseball people can talk about Cobb and Ruth and Mays (or whomever); tennis people can have a high time about Laver and Sampras; but in golf, there's nothing to discuss.

What's more, no one else was ever supposed to dominate the game. Nicklaus was supposed to be the last giant, the last player ever to make the others quake, the last to win predictably. You see, "parity" had arrived: That was the big buzzword on Tour. There were now thirty, forty—maybe sixty guys who could win in any given week. Golf instruction—swing science—had equalized things. Advances in equipment had equalized things. Conditioning, nutrition, etc., had equalized things. If a guy won, say, three tournaments in a season, that would be practically a freak, and the fellow would be Player of the Year, for sure. We would never see anything close to Nicklaus again.

Furthermore, his mark of 18 professional majors—twenty majors, if you counted his two U.S. Amateurs (and most of us did, because we loved that round, awesome number)—was an inviolable record. It would stand forever. It was the most unapproachable record in golf.

All of this needs to be remembered, because people forget. I've seen this in my own (not terribly long) lifetime. When I was young, the greatest record in baseball—the one that would live unto eternity—was Lou Gehrig's 2,130 consecutive games. That, all the experts said, was the one mark no one would ever reach. But then, when Cal Ripken closed in on it, they changed. They cheated. Now they said it was Joe D's 56-game hitting streak that was numero uno. Ah, but I remember: I won't forget. Ripken's achievement must not be slighted—everyone said it was impossible.

And now Tiger: The non-golfer will simply have to trust me that no one was supposed to be able to do what Tiger has, in fact, done. His achievements are—or were—unimaginable. The question arises, Has Woods won the Grand Slam? I, for one, don't care: He has won something like it—four consecutive majors—and no one else has (forgetting Bobby Jones, in the "premodern" Slam). I vow not to forget—no matter how fuzzy the past becomes—that Woods has accomplished what was proclaimed by one and all unaccomplishable.

How to talk about Tiger Woods? I don't know. Start with this (a cliche, but a useful cliche): When Nicklaus first showed up at the Masters, Bob Jones said, "He plays a game with which I am not familiar." The same has to be said of Woods. Another friend of mine—a pro golfer and a genuine philosophe—made the following, arresting statement: "It's not just that Woods is the best ever to play the game; it is that he is the first ever to play it." Think about that for more than a second or two, and you grow dizzy. What does it mean? It means, I think, that Tiger is the first truly to exploit the possibilities of the game. That he is the first to swing the club as it ought to be swung. That he—this gets a bit mystical—sees a game that others have been blind to, or have caught only glimpses of.

In the last years of his life, I had lessons—and many long conversations—with Bill Strausbaugh Jr., the most decorated teacher in the history of the PGA. "Coach" was one of the wisest men I ever hope to meet in golf, or to meet, period. Speaking of Tiger—this was in 1998, I believe—he said, "That young man has the best golf motion ever." (Coach disdained the word "swing"—he thought it gave his students the wrong idea.) I replied, condescendingly, like an idiot, "Oh, Coach, you must mean that he has one of the best ever. You've seen Hogan, Snead—all of them." He fixed me with a look and said, "No, Jay, I meant what I said: Tiger has the best golf motion ever." I was tremendously impressed by this, because the old are usually afflicted with the vice of nostalgia: No one is ever as good now as then. Thus, in baseball, for example, you hear, "Yeah, Roger Clemens is okay, but Grover Alexander! There was a pitcher!" Right.

Bill Strausbaugh also said, "Tiger has three things: a great golf motion, a great golf mind, and a great golf body. [This last, Coach maintained, is grossly underrated.] He is ideal—I never thought I would see it."

Tiger Woods was a legend before he ever turned pro. He had, I would argue, the greatest amateur career ever. (Bobby Jones idolaters—of whom I am one, from the crib—should just sit still. There is an argument here. And Jones wasn't an "amateur" in our present sense.) In fact, it's unfortunate about Tiger's dazzling pro career that it has been allowed to overshadow, inevitably, his amateur career. Tiger Woods, starting when he was 15 years old, won three straight U.S. Junior Championships and three straight U.S. Amateur Championships. This achievement is positively stupefying. I could try to explain, but, again, I say: Trust me.

Tiger was the youngest ever to win the Junior—he was 15. No one had ever won twice, and he would win three times. He was the youngest ever to win the U.S. Amateur—he was 18. He would be the only player ever to win the Am three years in a row. This takes a discipline, a kind of genius, that is hard to fathom. I argued, quite seriously, that if, God forbid, Tiger died before he ever had a chance to tee it up as a pro, he would die as one of the finest players in history. And he would have.

(I should interject here that Tiger—it is almost an afterthought—won the NCAA championship. He attended college—Stanford—for two years. Condoleezza Rice once told me—she had been provost of Stanford—that it was a shame that Tiger left school, understandable as it was, because he "really enjoyed it.")

Then there is Tiger the pro. Once more, how to convey the uniqueness—the impossibility—of it all? Tiger is only 25—and he has won 27 tournaments, including six majors (nine, if you count the way we do for Nicklaus). To provide a little comparison, Curtis Strange, who was the best player in the world for several years, won 17 tournaments, and two majors. At one stage, Woods won six PGA events in a row:

Farewell, parity. Indeed, before Woods, it was absurd to say, "I think so-and-so will win this golf tournament," or even, "So-and-so is the favorite." Golf is not a football game, in which one team or the other must win. Tiger has introduced a strange element: predictability.

Let's grapple with some victory margins: In 1997 (at age 21, but that's a different matter), Tiger won the Masters by twelve shots. I once heard the TV commentator Ken Venturi, in the pre-Tiger era, say of a guy who was leading some tournament by three shots—three shots—"He's lapping the field." And he was. When you win the Masters, you win it by one shot, two shots—three shots, maybe. Often, you're forced to win it in a sudden-death playoff. Tiger won the 1997 Masters by twelve shots: He could have made a 15 at the final par 4 and still won—could have made 16 to play off.

In 2000, he won the U.S. Open, at Pebble Beach, by fifteen shots. He won the British Open, at St. Andrews, by eight shots. (These are all records, but we can't possibly begin to go into the record book.) I argued—only half-jokingly, or a third jokingly—that Tiger should retire then and there, rather as Bobby Jones did, at age 28. What did he have left to prove? Sure, he had dreamed all his life of breaking Nicklaus's lifetime records, but that was just a matter of longevity, of hanging around, of staying uninjured, of keeping oneself interested. What is there left to do after winning the U.S. Open at Pebble (by fifteen) and the British at St. Andrews (by eight), and in the millennial year of 2000?

Well, you can go on to win a type of Slam, I guess. And Woods is still charging.

Of course, he is more than a golfer: He is an important American, not least because of the racial or ethnic question. There is probably no one in the country more refreshing, more resolute about race than Tiger Woods. He is a one-man army against cant and stupidity. One of the most thrilling television moments I have ever seen occurred at the Masters, when Tiger was playing as an amateur. Jim Nantz of CBS asked him one of those softball, standard, perfunctory questions: "Do you think you have an obligation to be a role model for minority kids?" Tiger answered, quick as a flash, "No." I almost fell out of my chair. He continued, "I have an obligation to be a role model for all kids."

After Tiger won the Masters in '97, President Clinton asked him, the morning after, to join him the following day, to participate in a Jackie Robinson ceremony at Shea Stadium. Tiger said . . . no, to the President of the United States. The invitation was last-minute, and Tiger was suspicious of its motives. He had long planned a vacation in Mexico with friends, and he wouldn't scrap or alter it. Many people criticized Tiger for this decision; but he told them, essentially, to get lost. Here was a firm, self-confident democratic citizen, not a serf, complying with the ruler's summons. The same mettle Woods shows on the golf course, he shows off it.

A good number of people don't like Tiger's attitude— don't like it at all. Larry King asked him, in 1998, "Do you feel that you're an influence on young blacks?" Tiger answered, calmly, unmovably, "Young children." An annoyed King shot back, "Just 'young children'? Don't you think you've attracted a lot more blacks to the game?" Replied Woods, "Yeah, I think I've attracted minorities to the game, but you know what? Why limit it to just that? I think you should be able to influence people in general, not just one race or social-economic background. Everybody should be in the fold." Again, I almost fell out of my chair. Tiger may be the most pointed universalist in public life.

Even Colin Powell, the current secretary of state, has gotten snippy with Tiger, or about him. Woods coined a word to describe his racial makeup: "Cablinasian." This is meant to stand for a mixture of Caucasian, black, Indian (American Indian), and Asian. Tiger's dad, a tough, no-nonsense career military man, is (to be disgustingly racial, but this is to make a point) half black, a quarter Chinese, and a quarter Indian; Tiger's mom is half Thai, a quarter Chinese, and a quarter white. Tiger is, in other words, 100 percent, pure American. Back to General Powell. On *Meet the Press* one Sunday in 1997, Tim Russert asked him (rather in the manner of Orval Faubus, actually), "If you have an ounce of black blood, aren't you black?" Powell responded that, like Tiger, he was of varied background, but "in order to not come up with a very strange word such as Tiger did, I consider myself black American. I'm very proud of it."

Well, despite his distaste for racial baloney, so is Woods: He is neither unaware nor unappreciative of the struggles of black people in this country. After winning the Masters that first time, he paid due homage to black players before him, including Charlie Sifford and Lee Elder (the first black to be allowed to play in the Masters, in 1975).

Yet Woods refuses to spend his life in obeisance to the race gods. At one point, he felt obliged to put out a "Media Statement," the purpose of which was "to explain my heritage." It would be—this is typical Tiger—"the final and only comment I will make regarding the issue":

> My parents have taught me to always be proud of my ethnic background. Please rest assured that is, and always will be, the case . . . On my father's side, I am African-American. On my mother's side, I am Thai. Truthfully, I feel very fortunate, and EQUALLY PROUD, to be both African-American and Asian!
>
> The critical and fundamental point is that ethnic background and/or composition should NOT make a difference. It does NOT make a difference to me. The bottom line is that I am an American . . . and proud of it! That is who I am and what I am. Now, with your cooperation, I hope I can just be a golfer and a human being.

We're told that we shouldn't need heroes. Well, too bad: We got one.

Not every touring pro has been gracious about Tiger and what he means; envy and resentment run deep. But the Scottish champion Colin Montgomerie said a lot when he commented recently, "We never thought this would happen [Tiger's explosion] or that there was even a chance it would happen. We're fortunate to have the world's best athlete playing our game. We're all not bad. He's just better. He is magnificent in every department."

Yes, in every department. A rare spirit shoots through Tiger. Consider a few, disparate things. Every year at Augusta, the Champions Dinner is held, for which the previous year's winner selects the menu. In 1998, Tiger—age 22—chose hamburgers and milkshakes: the all-American meal. After he won the '97 Masters (remember, by a historic twelve shots), he took a look at the film and announced, "My swing stinks" (he didn't say "stinks," but I've cleaned it up a little). So he worked to make it even better—and it may become better yet. Woods is a perfect combination of the cool, self-contained golfer, a la Ben Hogan (or Nicklaus, for that matter), and the hot, impassioned golfer, a la Arnold Palmer, or Seve Ballesteros. And, finally, there is no better interview in sports: He handles himself superbly, and is not above displaying a contempt (usually sly) for dumb questions.

My golf friends and I have made our peace with Tiger, to say the least. Initially, I think we all had a fear of his displacing Nicklaus, which seemed . . . sacrilegious. It helped, however, that Woods is the biggest Nicklaus worshiper of all: He venerates him as Nicklaus venerated Jones, and as Nicklaus pledged to follow in Jones's footsteps, Tiger has pledged to follow in Nicklaus's. Said Nicklaus five years ago, "There isn't a flaw in [Tiger's] golf or in his makeup. He will win more majors than Arnold Palmer and me [Arnie was standing next to him] combined. Somebody is going to dust my records. It might as well be Tiger, because he's such a great kid."

Oh, it's a thrill to be alive in the Time of Tiger. Whether you give a hoot about golf or not, I ask you—a final time—to trust me: Rejoice.

National Review, April 30, 2001

NOW, BEING GREAT ISN'T GOOD ENOUGH

Michael Wilbon

We're spoiled, all of us. We're as bad as the superstars we admonish. We don't know what greatness looks like anymore. We who follow sports, whether casually or fanatically, do not appreciate the concept of a "career year" or a feat being "once-in-a-lifetime." If Ted Williams had hit .400 in 2000, we'd be downright disappointed if he didn't hit .405 this year. If Wilt had scored his 100-point game in 1999, we'd be disappointed if he hadn't done it again by now.

That brings me to Tiger Woods, a man who has spent much of the summer in "a slump," who has been having "a disappointing year by his standards," who has "come back to the pack," and who, to hear some insiders tell it, has lost some of his aura since winning the Masters in April.

Collectively, let's get a grip.

The only thing wrong with the year Tiger's having is it isn't last year. And last year, most reasonable people concluded, was most likely a once-in-a-lifetimer. So anything less than last year is a slump? Has the culture surrounding sports become that extremist and unreasonable?

Did you catch the final round and the sudden-death playoff from Firestone Country Club on Sunday? It was the fifth PGA Tour victory of the season for a guy who celebrated his fifth year as a pro golfer yesterday. Throw in a win on the European Tour and that's six victories this year.

You know who else has won six? Nobody. Five? Nobody. Four? Nobody. Three? Nobody. Phil Mickleson, Scott Hoch, Sergio Garcia, David Toms and Joe Durant have won twice on tour this year. David Duval and Davis Love III have won once. Ernie Els, Vijay Singh and Justin Leonard have won major tournaments, but nothing else.

You want quality of wins? Tiger won arguably the most prestigious of the majors, the Masters. And beyond that he won The Players Championship, Bay Hill, The Memorial, and World Golf's NEC Invitational. Tell me Mickleson, Duval or Love wouldn't trade for that now? The only players on tour who can match Tiger's percentage of top–10 finishes (56 percent) are Mickleson, Singh and Love.

The guys on tour are lucky Tiger is just a fraction off. If anything, his ability to come back The Year After and win twice as many tournaments as anybody else while struggling, relatively, with his swing at times is doubly impressive. It's like he followed up a .406 season by hitting .391.

I should admit right here that I've been part of this stupid greed, of taking greatness for granted. Watching the beginning of Sunday's fourth round with some friends, I used the word "slump" to describe Tiger's summer. It's the second time in one year we've thrown around the word "slump" regarding Tiger. And my friend, Chris Cowan, reminded me Tiger had already won twice as many tournaments and twice as much money as anybody else and in a very real sense probably wasn't as far off his 2000 Tiger Slam form as we all seem to think.

And all you have to do is look at the stats. Okay, there are a couple of places where Tiger is noticeably down. Greens-in-regulation (75 percent to 71), driving accuracy (71 percent to 67) and holes per eagle (72 to 96) are all down. But look what happens when we move to more bottom-line numbers: To hear even Tiger tell it, he hasn't made a putt all summer, yet his putting average is down so slightly, from 1.717 putts per green to 1.763. Last year he averaged a tour-leading 4.92 birdies per round to 4.44 this year, which puts him No. 2. And while he averaged 67.79 strokes per round last year, he's scrambling around in 68.62 this year. First last year, first again this year. Poor Tiger.

This isn't just about Tiger and golf, though. Look at major league baseball. How blasé have we become regarding home runs. Okay, there were a few years there when the ball was clearly juiced and everybody and his mamma hit 50. But that was a while ago. Even with these small parks and inadequate depth in the pitching ranks, when a man hits more than 50 home runs, it's something that ought to make us stand and applaud. Even if they're hit late at night, say, in San Francisco, and by somebody whose everyday demeanor suggests he has visited the dentist's office every single morning of his life before he comes to work (Barry Bonds).

Maybe now that Sammy Sosa has joined the race and pulled within five home runs of Bonds, we'll become a little less casual about it. I understand that there's not the same fanfare about possibly hitting more than 60 that we had three years ago. A three-year-old record doesn't compare to a 37-year-old record. But for guys to be approaching the mid–50s in late-August is a stunning accomplishment. Bonds's sour puss doesn't change that. Who needs his sound bites? I don't want to hear Bonds talk, I want to see him swing. That Bonds is so disagreeable and obnoxious half his teammates hate him makes the whole thing spicier.

Of course, Woods never seems to be involved in a season-long chase because nobody can keep up. On Sunday he has the occasional duel, whether with Bob May or Jim Furyk, that makes for compelling TV. But from start to finish, he's so peerless and ahead of the field, we've started to yawn when his summer is less than unprecedented. Certainly, that says more about us than him.

Washington Post, August 28, 2001

TIGER WOODS TIMELINE

1975

Woods is born on Dec. 30 in Southern California, the son of Earl and Kultida Woods.

1976

After watching his father practicing in the garage, Woods tries to imitate his swing and his father gives him a cut-down club to practice with.

1977

Woods begins practicing at a driving range with his father and plays an occasional hole at the Navy Golf Club in Cypress, California.

1978

Woods is featured on a Los Angeles local news broadcast. Sportscaster and former pro football player Jim Hill comments, "That young man is going to be to golf what Jimmy Connors and Chris Evert are to tennis." He then appears on the Mike Douglas Show and gives a putting demonstration with Douglas and guests Bob Hope and Jimmy Stewart. After missing several times, he picks the ball up and drops it into the cup. Competes and wins a ten-and-under 9-hole tournament.

1979

Shoots a 48 over nine holes at the Navy Golf Club.

1981

Shoots a 57 over eighteen holes at the Heartwell Golf Park. Appears on ABC's "That's Incredible" television program and in a brief feature story in the November issue of *Golf Digest*.

1982

Featured in *Ebony* magazine. Competes in first major junior tournament, the Optimist International Junior Championship, finishing 8th in a field of 150.

1984

He wins the Optimist International Junior Championship, a title he would subsequently win five more times by age 15.

1990

Appears as a "Face in the Crowd" in *Sports Illustrated* on September 24.

1991

Wins the U.S. Junior Amateur, becoming the youngest champion in the history of the event.

1992

Wins the U.S. Junior National Championship and competes in his first professional event, the Nissan Los Angeles Open.

1993

Repeats as U.S. Junior National Champion, the first golfer to win the event twice.

1994

Wins the U.S. Amateur Championship at the Tournament Players Club at Sawgrass, becoming the youngest champion ever. Enrolls at Stanford University and joins the golf team.

1995

Defends title as U.S. Amateur Champion and is named NCAA First Team All-American. He participates in his first Master's tournament and ties for 41st place, the only amateur to make the cut.

1996

Becomes the first golfer in history to win three consecutive U.S. Amateur titles. Wins the NCAA individual men's championship. Competes as amateur in the Master's and U.S. Open. Decides to leave college and becomes a professional on August 27, competing in the Greater Milwaukee Open. He finishes 60th. He wins two of the eight tournaments in which he competes – the Las Vegas International for his first professional championship, and the Disney/Oldsmobile Classic.

1997

At age twenty-one he is the leading money winner on the PGA Tour with a record $2,066,833 in earnings. Wins first major championship, the Masters, by an amazing 12 strokes, the widest margin of victory in history, and also becomes the youngest-ever winner of the tournament. He also wins the Mercedes, Byron Nelson Classic, and Western Open.

1998

Wins the BellSouth Classic and makes the cut in 19 of 20 tournaments played, finishing in the top five eight times. Achieves number one world ranking.

1999

Finishes in the top ten in sixteen of twenty-one PGA tournaments. Wins the PGA championship by one stroke over Sergio Garcia. Also wins the Buick Invitational, Memorial, Western Open, WGC-NEC Invitational, the Disney Championship, Tour Championship and American Express Championship. Member of the winning U.S. Ryder Cup Team.

2000

Finishes in the top five in seventeen of twenty PGA tournaments. Wins the Mercedes Championship and AT&T Pebble Beach National Pro-Am for his fifth and sixth consecutive wins. Wins the U.S. Open at Pebble Beach by a record 15 strokes, the largest margin of victory ever recorded at a major tournament. Becomes the fifth player in history and the youngest to complete the career Grand Slam by winning the British Open with a 19-under 269, a record at St. Andrews and the lowest score ever in relation to par at a major tournament. Defeats Bob May in a three-hole playoff at Valhalla to win his second consecutive PGA Championship and third consecutive major title. He also wins the Bay Hill Invitational, Memorial, WGC-NEC Invitational and Canadian Open.

2001

Wins the Masters tournament to complete the "Tiger Slam," becoming the first golfer to ever hold the championship of all four majors at the same time. Also wins the Bay Hill Invitational, Players Championship, the Memorial, and WGC-NEC Invitational.

LIST OF CONTRIBUTORS

Thomas Boswell is a columnist for the *Washington Post* and author of many books, among them *Why Time Begins on Opening Day* and *Strokes of Genius*.

Frank Deford appears regularly on NPR's *Morning Edition* and is author of *The Best of Frank Deford*.

Ron Fimrite was a senior writer for *Sports Illustrated* and is the author of *Birth of Fan*.

Peter de Jonge is coauthor with James Patterson of *Miracle on the 17th Green*.

Jaime Diaz is the author of *Hallowed Ground: Golf's Greatest Places*.

Maureen Dowd is a columnist for the *New York Times*, and in 1999 won the Pulitzer Prize for commentary.

James K. Glassman is currently resident fellow, American Enterprise Institute, and host, TechCentralStation.com.

Ellen Goodman is a syndicated columnist and coauthor of *I Know Just What You Mean*.

Dan Jenkins's latest novel is *The Money-Whipped Steer-Job Three-Jack Give-Up Artist*.

Erin Aubry Kaplan is a staff writer for *LA Weekly*.

Dave Kindred is a contributing writer for *The Sporting News*.

Tony Kornheiser is a columnist for the *Washington Post* and author of *Pumping Irony* and *Bald As I Want to Be*.

James Lawton is a sports columnist for the *Independent* and author of *Mission Impossible*.

Robert Lipsyte is a sports columnist for the *New York Times* and author of *In the Country of Illness*.

Hugh McIllvanney is one of England's preeminent sports writers.

The late **Jim Murray** of the *Los Angeles Times* won the Pulitzer Prize for commentary in 1988.

Jay Nordlinger is managing editor of the *National Review*.

Charles P. Pierce is writer-at-large for *Esquire* and author of the collection *Sports Guy*.

Gary Smith of *Sports Illustrated* is the author of *Beyond the Game: The Collected Sportswriting of Gary Smith*.

Michael Wilbon is a sports columnist for the *Washington Post*.

CREDITS

"Fore! Nicklaus Beware of Teen-Ager" by Jaime Diaz, *New York Times*, August 1, 1991. Reprinted by permission of the author.

"A Zone of His Own" by Peter de Jonge, *New York Times Magazine*, February 5, 1995. Reprinted by permission of the author.

"Challenging the Categories" by Ellen Goodman, *Boston Globe*, April 13, 1995. Copyright © 1995, The Boston Globe Newspaper Co./Washington Post Writers Group. Reprinted by permission.

"Five Above Par" by Ron Fimrite, *Stanford Alumni Magazine*, June 1995. Reprinted by permission of the author.

"A Dishonest Ad Campaign" by James K. Glassman, *Washington Post*, September 17, 1996. Reprinted by permission of the author.

"The Chosen One" by Gary Smith, *Sports Illustrated*, December 23, 1996. Reprinted courtesy of *Sports Illustrated*. Copyright © 1996, Time Inc. All rights reserved.

"So Young to Have the Master's Touch" by Dave Kindred, *The Sporting News*, April 21, 1997. Reprinted by permission of *The Sporting News*.

"Tiger Woods Goes for the Green" by Maureen Dowd, *New York Times*, April 22, 1997. Copyright © 1997 by the New York Times Co. Reprinted by permission.

"The Man, Amen" by Charles P. Pierce, GQ, April 1997. Reprinted by permission of the author.

"The Lost Generation" by Frank Deford, *Newsweek*, June 2, 1997. Copyright © 1997 Newsweek, Inc. All rights reserved. Reprinted by permission.

"Wait! It's Not Supposed to End This Way, Is It?" by Jim Murray, *Los Angeles Times*, March 2, 1998. Copyright © Los Angeles Times. Reprinted with permission.

"Falling for Tiger Woods" by Erin Aubry Kaplan, *Salon*, October 1, 1998. Reprinted by permission of the author.

"A Club of One" by Thomas Boswell, *Washington Post*, June 18, 2000. Copyright © 2000, The Washington Post. Reprinted with permission.

"With the Course He's On, Things Can Only Get Better" by Thomas Boswell, *Washington Post*, June 19, 2000. Copyright © 2000, The Washington Post. Reprinted with permission.

"Tiger's Triumph" by Tony Kornheiser, *Washington Post*, June 20, 2000. Copyright © 2000, The Washington Post. Reprinted with permission.

"A Genius Comfortable with His Gifts" by Hugh McIllvanney, *Times of London*, July 7, 2000. Copyright © Times Newspapers Limited, 2000.

"The Greatest" by James Lawton, *The Independent*, August 22, 2000. Reprinted by permission of *The Independent*.